bowl
food

bowl food

MURDOCH BOOKS

Contents

Soups

Spicy pumpkin and coconut soup

1 small fresh red chilli, seeded and
chopped
1 stem lemon grass, white part only,
sliced
1 teaspoon ground coriander
1 tablespoon chopped fresh ginger
2 cups (500 ml) vegetable stock
2 tablespoons oil
1 onion, finely chopped
800 g pumpkin flesh, cubed
(see Note)
1½ cups (375 ml) coconut milk
3 tablespoons chopped fresh
coriander leaves
2 teaspoons shaved palm sugar
or soft brown sugar
extra coriander leaves, to garnish

Place the chilli, lemon grass, ground
coriander, ginger and 2 tablespoons
vegetable stock in a food processor,
and process until smooth.

Heat the oil in a large saucepan, add
the onion and cook over medium heat
for 5 minutes. Add the spice paste
and cook, stirring, for 1 minute.

Add the pumpkin and remaining
vegetable stock. Bring to the boil,
then reduce the heat and simmer,
covered, for 15–20 minutes, or until
the pumpkin is tender. Cool slightly
then process in a food processor
or blender until smooth. Return to
the cleaned pan, stir in the coconut
milk, coriander and palm sugar, and
simmer until hot. Garnish with the
extra coriander leaves.

Serves 4

Note: You will need to buy 1.5 kg
pumpkin with the skin on to yield
800 g flesh.

Miso soup with chicken and udon noodles

8 dried shiitake mushrooms
600 g chicken breast fillets, cut
   into 1.5 cm thick strips
1/4 cup (60 g) white miso paste
2 teaspoons dashi granules
1 tablespoon wakame flakes or other
   seaweed (see Note)
300 g baby bok choy, halved
   lengthways
400 g fresh udon noodles
150 g silken firm tofu, cut into
   1 cm cubes
3 spring onions, sliced diagonally

Soak the mushrooms in 1 cup
(250 ml) boiling water for 20 minutes.
Drain, reserving the liquid; discard
the stalks and thinly slice the caps.

Pour 2 litres water into a saucepan
and bring to the boil, then reduce
the heat and simmer. Add the chicken
and cook for 2–3 minutes, or until
almost cooked through.

Add the mushrooms and cook for
1 minute, then add the miso paste,
dashi granules, wakame and reserved
mushroom liquid. Stir to dissolve the
dashi and miso paste. Do not boil.

Add the bok choy halves and simmer
for 1 minute, or until beginning to wilt,
then add the noodles and simmer for
a further 2 minutes. Gently stir in the
tofu and ladle the hot soup into large
serving bowls. Garnish with the sliced
spring onion.

Serves 4–6

Note: Wakame is a curly-leafed,
brown algae with a mild vegetable
taste and a soft texture. It can be
used in salads or can be boiled and
served like a vegetable. Use a small
amount as it swells by about ten
times after being cooked.

Tomato bread soup

750 g vine-ripened tomatoes
1 loaf (450 g) day-old crusty Italian
  bread
1 tablespoon olive oil
3 cloves garlic, crushed
1 tablespoon tomato paste
1.25 litres hot vegetable stock
4 tablespoons torn fresh basil leaves
2–3 tablespoons extra virgin olive oil
extra virgin olive oil, extra, to serve

Score a cross in the base of each tomato. Place in a bowl of boiling water for 1 minute, then plunge into cold water and peel the skin away from the cross. Cut the tomatoes in half and scoop out the seeds with a teaspoon. Chop the tomato flesh.

Remove most of the crust from the bread and discard. Cut the bread into 3 cm pieces.

Heat the oil in a large saucepan. Add the garlic, tomato and tomato paste, then reduce the heat and simmer, stirring occasionally, for 10–15 minutes, or until reduced and thickened. Add the stock and bring to the boil, stirring for 2–3 minutes. Reduce the heat to medium, add the bread pieces and cook, stirring, for 5 minutes, or until the bread softens and absorbs most of the liquid. Add more stock or water if necessary.

Stir in the torn basil leaves and extra virgin olive oil, and leave for 5 minutes so the flavours have time to develop. Drizzle with a little extra virgin olive oil.

Serves 4

Five-spice duck and somen noodle soup

4 duck breasts, skin on
1 teaspoon five-spice powder
1 teaspoon peanut oil
200 g dried somen noodles

Star anise broth
1 litre chicken stock
3 whole star anise
5 spring onions, chopped
¼ cup (5 g) chopped fresh
   coriander leaves

Preheat the oven to moderately hot 200°C (400°F/Gas 6). Trim the duck breast of excess fat, then lightly sprinkle both sides with the five-spice powder.

Heat the oil in a large frying pan. Add the duck skin-side down and cook over medium heat for 2–3 minutes, or until brown and crisp. Turn and cook the other side for 3 minutes. Transfer to a baking tray and cook, skin-side up, for another 8–10 minutes, or until cooked to your liking.

Meanwhile, place the chicken stock and star anise in a small saucepan. Bring to the boil, then reduce the heat and simmer for 5 minutes. Add the spring onion and coriander and simmer for 5 minutes.

Cook the noodles in a saucepan of boiling water for 2 minutes, or until soft. Drain and divide among four bowls. Ladle the broth on the noodles and top each bowl with one sliced duck breast.

Serves 4

Beef and beet borscht

2 tablespoons olive oil
1 onion, chopped
2 cloves garlic, crushed
500 g beef chuck steak, cut into
 2 cm cubes
1 litre beef stock
2 small beetroot (250 g)
200 g canned crushed tomatoes
1 carrot, diced
2 potatoes (280 g), diced
2½ cups (190 g) finely shredded
 cabbage
2 teaspoons lemon juice
2 teaspoons sugar
2 tablespoons chopped fresh
 flat-leaf parsley
2 tablespoons chopped fresh dill
⅓ cup (90 g) sour cream

Preheat the oven to moderately hot 200°C (400°F/Gas 6). Heat the oil in a large saucepan, and cook the onion and garlic over medium heat for 3–5 minutes. Add the beef, stock and 1 litre water, and bring to the boil. Reduce the heat and simmer, covered, for 1 hour 15 minutes, or until the meat is tender. Remove the meat.

Trim the beetroot just above the end of the leaf stalks. Wrap in foil and bake for 30–40 minutes, or until tender. Unwrap and leave to cool.

Return the stock to the boil and add the tomato, carrot and potato, and season with salt. Cook over medium heat for 10 minutes. Add the cabbage and cook for 5 minutes. Peel and dice the beetroot. Return the meat to the pan and add the beetroot, lemon juice, sugar and 1½ tablespoons each of parsley and dill. Cook for 2 minutes, or until heated through. Season to taste.

Remove from the heat and leave for 10 minutes. Serve with a dollop of sour cream and garnish with the remaining dill and parsley.

Serves 4

Prawn laksa

1½ tablespoons coriander seeds
1 tablespoon cumin seeds
1 teaspoon ground turmeric
1 onion, roughly chopped
1 cm x 3 cm piece fresh ginger,
   peeled and roughly chopped
3 cloves garlic
3 stems lemon grass, white part only,
   sliced
6 macadamia nuts
4–6 small fresh red chillies
2–3 teaspoons shrimp paste
1 litre chicken stock
¼ cup (60 ml) oil
3 cups (750 ml) coconut milk
4 fresh kaffir lime leaves
2½ tablespoons lime juice
2 tablespoons fish sauce
2 tablespoons grated palm sugar
   or soft brown sugar
750 g raw medium prawns, peeled
   and deveined, with tails intact
250 g dried rice vermicelli noodles
1 cup (90 g) bean sprouts
4 fried tofu puffs, julienned
3 tablespoons roughly chopped
   fresh Vietnamese mint
⅔ cup (20 g) fresh coriander leaves
lime wedges, to serve

Dry-roast the coriander seeds over medium heat for 1–2 minutes, or until fragrant, tossing constantly to prevent burning. Grind in a mortar and pestle or a spice grinder. Repeat with the cumin seeds. Place all of the spices, onion, ginger, garlic, lemon grass, macadamias, chillies and shrimp paste in a blender, add ½ cup (125 ml) of stock and blend to a paste.

Heat the oil over low heat and cook the paste for 3–5 minutes, stirring constantly to prevent it burning or sticking. Add the remaining stock, bring to the boil, then reduce the heat and simmer for 15 minutes, or until reduced slightly. Add the coconut milk, lime leaves, lime juice, fish sauce and palm sugar, and simmer for 5 minutes. Add the prawns and simmer for 2 minutes, or until they are pink and cooked through. Do not boil or cover.

Soak the vermicelli in boiling water for 5 minutes, or until soft. Drain and divide among serving bowls with most of the sprouts. Ladle hot soup over the noodles and garnish each bowl with tofu, mint, coriander leaves and the remaining bean sprouts. Serve with lime wedges.

Serves 4–6

Caramelised onion and parsnip soup

30 g butter
3 large onions, halved and thinly
  sliced
2 tablespoons firmly packed soft
  brown sugar
1 cup (250 ml) dry white wine
3 large parsnips, peeled, chopped
1.25 litres vegetable stock
¼ cup (60 ml) cream
fresh thyme leaves, to garnish

Melt the butter in a large saucepan. Add the onion and sugar, and cook over low heat for 10 minutes. Add the wine and parsnip, and simmer, covered, for 20 minutes, or until the onion and parsnip are golden and tender.

Pour in the stock, bring to the boil, then reduce the heat and simmer, covered, for 10 minutes. Cool slightly, then place in a blender or food processor and blend in batches until smooth. Season. Drizzle with a little cream and sprinkle fresh thyme leaves over the top. Serve with toasted crusty bread slices.

Serves 4

Thai-style chicken and coconut soup

2 stems lemon grass, white part finely
   chopped, stem ends reserved and
   halved
6 cloves garlic, chopped
3 red Asian shallots, chopped
8 black peppercorns
1 teaspoon ready-made red curry
   paste
1 cup (250 ml) coconut cream
400 ml coconut milk
400 ml chicken stock
2½ tablespoons thinly sliced fresh
   galangal
7 kaffir lime leaves, shredded
400 g chicken breast fillets or thigh
   fillets, thinly sliced
2 tablespoons lime juice
2 tablespoons fish sauce
1 teaspoon grated palm sugar or soft
   brown sugar
3 tablespoons fresh coriander leaves
1 small fresh red chilli, thinly sliced

Process the chopped lemon grass,
garlic, shallots, peppercorns and
curry paste in a food processor
to form a paste.

Heat a wok over low heat, add
the coconut cream, increase the
heat to high and bring to the boil.
Add the paste and cook, stirring,
for 5 minutes. Add the coconut milk
and stock, return to the boil and add
the sliced galangal, the kaffir lime
leaves and reserved lemon grass
stems. Reduce the heat and simmer
for 5 minutes.

Add the chicken and simmer for
8 minutes, or until cooked. Stir
in the lime juice, fish sauce, palm
sugar, coriander leaves and chilli.
Serve immediately.

Serves 4

Rice noodle soup with duck

1 whole Chinese roast duck
4 fresh coriander roots and stems,
  well rinsed
5 slices fresh galangal
4 spring onions, sliced on the
  diagonal into 3 cm lengths
400 g Chinese broccoli, cut into
  5 cm lengths
2 cloves garlic, crushed
3 tablespoons fish sauce
1 tablespoon hoisin sauce
2 teaspoons grated palm sugar
  or soft brown sugar
½ teaspoon ground white pepper
500 g fresh rice noodles
crispy fried garlic flakes, to garnish,
  optional
fresh coriander leaves, to garnish,
  optional

To make the stock, cut off the duck's head with a sharp knife and discard. Remove the skin and fat, leaving the neck intact. Carefully remove the flesh from the bones and set aside. Cut any visible fat from the carcass along with the parson's nose, then discard. Break the carcass into large pieces, then place in a large stockpot with 2 litres water.

Bruise the coriander roots and stems with the back of a knife. Add to the pot with the galangal and bring to the boil. Skim off any foam from the surface. Boil over medium heat for 15 minutes. Strain the stock through a fine sieve, discard the carcass, and return the stock to a clean saucepan.

Slice the duck flesh into strips. Add to the stock with the spring onion, Chinese broccoli, garlic, fish sauce, hoisin sauce, palm sugar and white pepper. Gently bring to the boil.

Cook the noodles in boiling water for 2–3 minutes, or until tender. Drain well. Divide the noodles and soup evenly among the serving bowls. If desired, garnish with the garlic flakes and coriander leaves. Serve immediately.

Serves 4–6

Hearty bean and pasta soup

1 tablespoon olive oil
1 onion, finely chopped
3 cloves garlic, crushed
2 x 290 g cans mixed beans, drained
1.75 litres chicken stock (see Note)
100 g conchigliette pasta
1 tablespoon chopped fresh tarragon

Heat the oil in a saucepan over low heat. Add the onion and cook for 5 minutes, then add the garlic and cook for a further 1 minute, stirring frequently. Add the beans and chicken stock, cover the pan with a lid, increase the heat and bring to the boil. Add the pasta and cook until *al dente*. Stir in the tarragon, then season with salt and black pepper. Serve with crusty bread.

Serves 4

Note: The flavour of this soup is enhanced by using a good-quality stock. Either make your own or use the tetra packs of liquid stock that are available at the supermarket.

Prawn, potato and corn chowder

600 g raw medium prawns
3 corn cobs, husks removed
1 tablespoon olive oil
2 leeks, white part only, finely
   chopped
2 cloves garlic, crushed
650 g potatoes, cut into 1.5 cm
   cubes
3 cups (750 ml) fish or chicken stock
1½ cups (375 ml) milk
1 cup (250 ml) cream
pinch of cayenne pepper
3 tablespoons finely chopped fresh
   flat-leaf parsley

Peel and devein the prawns, then chop them into 1.5 cm pieces.

Cut the kernels from the corn cobs. Heat the oil in a large saucepan and add the leek. Cook over medium–low heat for about 5 minutes, or until soft and lightly golden. Add the garlic and cook for 30 seconds, then add the corn, potato, stock and milk.

Bring to the boil, then reduce the heat and simmer, partially covered, for about 20 minutes, or until the potato is soft but still holds its shape (it will break down slightly). Remove the lid and simmer for a further 10 minutes to allow the soup to thicken. Reduce the heat to low. Put 2 cups (500 ml) of the soup in a blender and blend until very smooth.

Return the blended soup to the saucepan and add the prawns. Increase the heat to medium and simmer for 2 minutes, or until the prawns are pink and cooked through. Stir in the cream, cayenne pepper and 2 tablespoons of the parsley. Season to taste with salt, then serve garnished with the remaining parsley.

Serves 4–6

Pea and rocket soup

1 tablespoon olive oil
1 red onion, finely chopped
700 g frozen peas
100 g rocket leaves
3 cups (750 ml) hot vegetable stock
shaved Parmesan, to garnish
rocket leaves, extra, to garnish

Heat the oil in a large saucepan over medium heat. Add the onion and cook for 5 minutes, or until soft. Add the peas and rocket, and cook for a further 2 minutes. Add the stock and 1 cup (250 ml) water, bring to the boil, then reduce the heat and simmer for 20 minutes.

Cool slightly then place in a food processor or blender in batches and process until almost smooth. Return to the cleaned saucepan and heat through. Serve garnished with shaved Parmesan and the extra rocket.

Serves 4

Vegetable ramen

375 g fresh ramen noodles
1 tablespoon oil
1 tablespoon finely chopped fresh
  ginger
2 cloves garlic, crushed
150 g oyster mushrooms, halved
1 small zucchini, sliced into thin
  rounds
1 leek, white and light green part,
  halved lengthways and thinly sliced
100 g snow peas, halved diagonally
100 g fried tofu puffs, cut into
  matchsticks
1.25 litres vegetable stock
1½ tablespoons white miso paste
2 tablespoons light soy sauce
1 tablespoon mirin
1 cup (90 g) bean sprouts
1 teaspoon sesame oil
4 spring onions, thinly sliced
100 g enoki mushrooms

Bring a large saucepan of lightly salted water to the boil. Add the noodles and cook, stirring to prevent sticking, for 4 minutes, or until just tender. Drain and rinse under cold running water.

Heat the oil in a large saucepan over medium heat, add the ginger, crushed garlic, oyster mushrooms, zucchini, leek, snow peas and tofu puffs, and stir-fry for 2 minutes. Add the stock and 300 ml water and bring to the boil, then reduce the heat and simmer. Stir in the miso, soy sauce and mirin until heated through. Do not boil. Stir in the bean sprouts and sesame oil.

Place the noodles in the bottom of six serving bowls, then pour in the soup. Garnish with the spring onion and enoki mushrooms.

Serves 6

Chicken and pumpkin laksa

Paste
2 birds eye chillies, seeded and
    roughly chopped
2 stems lemon grass, white part only,
    roughly chopped
4 red Asian shallots, peeled
1 tablespoon roughly chopped fresh
    ginger
1 teaspoon ground turmeric
3 candlenuts, optional

110 g dried rice noodle sticks
1 tablespoon peanut oil
250 g butternut pumpkin, cut into
    2 cm chunks
800 ml coconut milk
600 g chicken breast fillets, cut
    into cubes
2 tablespoons lime juice
1 tablespoon fish sauce
1 cup (90 g) bean sprouts
½ cup (15 g) torn fresh basil
½ cup (10 g) torn fresh mint
½ cup (50 g) unsalted peanuts,
    toasted and chopped
1 lime, cut into quarters

Place all the paste ingredients in
a food processor with 1 tablespoon
water and blend until smooth.

Soak the noodles in boiling water
for 15–20 minutes. Drain.

Meanwhile, heat the oil in a wok
and swirl to coat. Add the paste
and stir over low heat for 5 minutes,
or until aromatic. Add the pumpkin
and coconut milk and simmer for
10 minutes. Add the chicken and
simmer for 20 minutes. Stir in the
lime juice and fish sauce.

Divide the noodles among four
deep serving bowls, then ladle
the soup over them. Garnish with
the bean sprouts, basil, mint, peanuts
and lime.

Serves 4

Chickpea soup

1½ cups (330 g) dried chickpeas
½ brown onion
1 bay leaf
½ head garlic, unpeeled (8 cloves)
2 tablespoons olive oil
1 celery stick, chopped
1 large onion, extra, finely chopped
3 cloves garlic, extra, chopped
1 teaspoon ground cumin
1 teaspoon paprika
¼ teaspoon dried chilli powder
3 teaspoons chopped fresh oregano
1 litre vegetable stock
2 tablespoons lemon juice
olive oil, extra to drizzle

Place the chickpeas in a bowl and cover with water. Soak overnight, then drain. Transfer to a saucepan and add the onion, bay leaf, garlic and 1.5 litres water. Bring to the boil, then reduce the heat and simmer for 1 hour, or until the chickpeas are tender. Drain, reserving 2 cups (500 ml) cooking liquid. Discard the onion, bay leaf and garlic.

Heat the oil in the same saucepan, add the celery and extra onion, and cook over medium heat for 5 minutes, or until golden. Add the extra garlic and cook for a further 1 minute. Add the cumin, paprika, chilli powder and 2 teaspoons of the oregano, and cook, stirring, for 1 minute. Return the chickpeas to the pan and stir to coat with the spices.

Pour in the vegetable stock and reserved cooking liquid, bring to the boil, then reduce the heat and simmer for 20 minutes. Stir in the lemon juice and remaining oregano and serve drizzled with olive oil.

Serves 4

Crab and corn eggflower noodle broth

75 g dried thin egg noodles
1 tablespoon peanut oil
1 teaspoon finely chopped fresh
  ginger
3 spring onions, thinly sliced, white
  and green parts separated
1.25 litres chicken stock
1/3 cup (80 ml) mirin
250 g baby corn, sliced on the
  diagonal into 1 cm slices
175 g fresh crab meat
1 tablespoon cornflour mixed with
  1 tablespoon water
2 eggs, lightly beaten
2 teaspoons lime juice
1 tablespoon soy sauce
1/4 cup (7 g) torn fresh coriander
  leaves

Cook the noodles in boiling salted water for 3 minutes, or until just tender. Drain and rinse under cold water.

Heat the oil in a large heavy-based saucepan. Add the ginger and the spring onion (white part) and cook over medium heat for 1–2 minutes. Add the stock, mirin and corn and bring to the boil. Simmer for about 5 minutes. Stir in the noodles, crab meat and cornflour mixture. Return to a simmer, stirring constantly until it thickens. Reduce the heat and pour in the egg in a thin stream, stirring constantly—do not boil. Gently stir in the lime juice, soy sauce and half the coriander.

Divide the noodles among four bowls and ladle the soup on top. Garnish with the spring onion (green part) and coriander leaves.

Serves 4

Hot and sour prawn soup

350 g raw medium prawns
1 tablespoon oil
3 stems lemon grass, white part
  only
3 thin slices fresh galangal
3–5 small fresh red chillies
5 fresh kaffir lime leaves, finely
  shredded
2 tablespoons fish sauce
2 spring onions, sliced
½ cup (70 g) canned straw
  mushrooms, drained, or quartered
  button mushrooms
3 tablespoons lime juice
1–2 tablespoons chilli paste,
  or to taste
fresh coriander leaves, to garnish,
  optional

Peel and devein the prawns, leaving the tail intact and reserving the heads and shells. Heat the oil in a large stockpot or wok and add the prawn heads and shells. Cook for 5 minutes, or until the shells turn bright orange. Bruise 1 stem of the lemon grass with the back of a knife. Add to the pan with the galangal and 2 litres water. Bring to the boil, then reduce the heat and simmer for 20 minutes. Strain the stock and return to the pan. Discard the shells and herbs.

Finely slice the chillies and remaining lemon grass. Add to the liquid with the lime leaves, fish sauce, spring onion and mushrooms. Cook gently for 2 minutes.

Add the prawns and cook for 3 minutes, or until the prawns are tender. Add the lime juice and chilli paste (adjust to taste with extra lime juice or fish sauce). If desired, garnish with coriander leaves.

Serves 4–6

Notes: To add more flavour and depth, replace the water with chicken stock. Chilli paste with soy bean oil is sometimes called 'chilli jam' and is available from Asian food stores.

Sweet potato and pear soup

25 g butter
1 small white onion, finely chopped
750 g orange sweet potato, peeled
  and cut into 2 cm dice
2 firm pears (500 g), peeled, cored
  and cut into 2 cm dice
3 cups (750 ml) chicken or vegetable
  stock
1 cup (250 ml) cream
chopped fresh mint, to garnish

Melt the butter in a saucepan over medium heat, add the onion and cook for 2–3 minutes, or until softened but not brown. Add the sweet potato and pear, and cook, stirring, for 1–2 minutes. Add the stock to the pan, bring to the boil and cook for 20 minutes, or until the sweet potato and pear are soft.

Cool slightly, then place the mixture in a blender or food processor and blend in batches until smooth. Return to the pan, stir in the cream and gently reheat without boiling. Season with salt and ground black pepper. Garnish with the fresh mint.

Serves 4

Note: This soup can be frozen before you add the cream. To serve, defrost the soup, then gently reheat, stirring in the cream.

Beef pho

200 g rice noodle sticks
1.5 litres beef stock
1 star anise
4 cm piece fresh ginger, sliced
2 pigs trotters (ask your butcher
   to cut them in half)
1/2 onion, studded with 2 cloves
2 stems lemon grass, pounded
2 cloves garlic, pounded
1/4 teaspoon white pepper
1 tablespoon fish sauce
400 g beef fillet, partially frozen,
   and thinly sliced
1 cup (90 g) bean sprouts
2 spring onions, thinly sliced on
   the diagonal
1/2 cup (25 g) fresh coriander leaves,
   chopped
1/2 cup (25 g) fresh Vietnamese mint,
   chopped
1 fresh red chilli, thinly sliced
fresh red chillies, extra, to serve
fresh Vietnamese mint, extra, to serve
fresh coriander leaves, extra, to serve
2 limes, cut into quarters
fish sauce, extra, to serve

Soak the noodles in boiling water
for 15–20 minutes. Drain.

Bring the stock, star anise, ginger,
trotters, onion, lemon grass, garlic
and white pepper to the boil in a
large saucepan. Reduce the heat
and simmer for 30 minutes. Strain,
return to the same pan and stir in
the fish sauce.

Divide the noodles among bowls,
then top with beef strips, sprouts,
spring onion, coriander, mint and
chilli. Ladle on the broth.

Place the extra chilli, mint, coriander,
lime quarters and fish sauce in small
bowls on a platter, serve with the
soup and allow your guests to help
themselves.

Serves 4

Corn and lemon grass soup with yabbies

4 corn cobs
1 tablespoon oil
1 leek, white part only, chopped
1 celery stick, chopped
3 stems lemon grass, white part only, bruised
2 cloves garlic, crushed
1 teaspoon ground cumin
1 teaspoon ground coriander
3/4 teaspoon ground white pepper
3 kaffir lime leaves
3 cups (750 ml) chicken stock
800 ml coconut milk
1/2 cup (125 ml) cream
2 teaspoons butter
3 cloves garlic, crushed, extra
1/2 teaspoon sambal oelek
1.2 kg cooked yabbies or crayfish, peeled and shredded
1 tablespoon finely chopped fresh coriander leaves

Trim the kernels from the corn. Heat the oil over medium heat, add the leek, celery and lemon grass and stir for 10 minutes, or until the leek is soft. Add the garlic, cumin, coriander and 1/2 teaspoon of the pepper and cook, stirring, for 1–2 minutes, or until fragrant. Add the corn, lime leaves, stock and coconut milk, stir well and simmer, stirring occasionally, for 1 1/2 hours. Remove from the heat and cool slightly. Remove the lemon grass and lime leaves and blend the mixture in batches in a food processor until smooth.

Push the mixture through a sieve with a wooden spoon. Repeat. Return to a large, clean saucepan, add the cream, and warm gently.

Melt the butter in a frying pan over medium heat, add the extra garlic, sambal oelek, remaining pepper and a pinch of salt and stir for 1 minute. Add the yabby meat, stir for a further minute, or until heated through, then remove from the heat and stir in the fresh coriander.

Ladle the soup into shallow soup bowls, then pile some yabby meat in the centre of each bowl.

Serves 4 (6 as an entrée)

Green tea noodle soup

200 g dried green tea noodles
2 teaspoons dashi granules
1 tablespoon mirin
1 tablespoon Japanese soy sauce
200 g firm tofu, drained and cut into
   1.5 cm cubes
1 sheet nori, shredded
3 teaspoons toasted sesame seeds

Cook the noodles in a large saucepan of boiling salted water for 5 minutes, or until tender. Drain and rinse under cold water.

Combine the dashi granules with 1.5 litres water in a large saucepan. Stir over medium–high heat until the granules are dissolved. Increase the heat to high and bring to the boil. Stir in the mirin and soy sauce.

Divide the noodles and tofu cubes among four serving bowls and ladle the hot stock on top. Garnish with the nori and sesame seeds. Serve immediately.

Serves 4

Minestrone

2 cups (400 g) dried cannellini
  or borlotti beans
1 tablespoon olive oil
100 g mild pancetta, finely diced
1 onion, chopped
1 carrot, diced
2 sticks celery, diced
1 large potato, diced
2 cloves garlic, crushed
3 tablespoons tomato paste
2 x 425 g cans crushed tomatoes
3 cups (750 ml) beef stock
1 cup (155 g) elbow macaroni
  or ditalini
1 cup (75 g) shredded cabbage
2 tablespoons shredded fresh basil
shaved Parmesan, to serve
extra virgin olive oil, to serve

Place the beans in a large bowl, cover with cold water and leave to soak overnight.

Heat the oil in a large saucepan, add the pancetta and cook over medium heat, stirring, for 1–2 minutes, or until slightly crisp. Add the onion, carrot, celery, potato and garlic and cook for 1–2 minutes. Add the tomato paste, tomato, beef stock and drained beans. Bring to the boil, then reduce the heat and simmer, covered, for 40 minutes or until the beans are tender. (Do not add salt prior to this stage as it will toughen the beans.)

Add the pasta and cabbage, and cook for a further 15 minutes. Season with salt and black pepper. Serve in deep bowls with the basil, shaved Parmesan, a drizzle of extra virgin olive oil and wood-fired bread.

Serves 6

Sukiyaki soup

10 g dried sliced shiitake mushrooms
100 g dried rice vermicelli
2 teaspoons oil
1 leek, halved and sliced
1 litre chicken stock
1 teaspoon dashi granules dissolved
   in 2 cups (500 ml) boiling water
1/2 cup (125 ml) soy sauce
2 tablespoons mirin
1 1/2 tablespoons sugar
2 cups (100 g) shredded Chinese
   cabbage (wom buk)
300 g silken firm tofu, cut into 2 cm
   cubes
600 g rump steak, thinly sliced
4 spring onions, sliced diagonally

Soak the shiitake mushrooms in 1/2 cup (125 ml) boiling water for 10 minutes. Place the noodles in a large heatproof bowl, cover with boiling water and leave them to stand for 5 minutes, then drain.

Heat the oil in a large saucepan, add the leek and cook over medium heat for 3 minutes, or until softened. Add the chicken stock, dashi broth, soy sauce, mirin, sugar and mushrooms and their soaking liquid. Bring to the boil, then reduce the heat and simmer for 5 minutes.

Add the cabbage and simmer for a further 5 minutes. Next, add the tofu and beef, and simmer for 5 minutes, or until the beef is cooked but still tender. Divide the noodles among the serving bowls and ladle on the soup. Serve garnished with the spring onion.

Serves 4–6

Pea and ham soup

500 g yellow or green split peas
1½ tablespoons olive oil
2 onions, chopped
1 carrot, diced
3 sticks celery, finely chopped
1 kg ham bones or a smoked hock,
   chopped
1 bay leaf
2 sprigs fresh thyme
lemon juice, to taste (optional)

Place the peas in a large bowl, cover with cold water and soak for 6 hours. Drain well. Heat the oil in a large saucepan, add the onion, carrot and celery, and cook over low heat for 6–7 minutes, or until vegetables are soft but not brown.

Add the split peas, ham bones, bay leaf, thyme and 2.5 litres cold water, and bring to the boil. Reduce the heat and simmer, stirring occasionally, for 2 hours, or until the peas are tender. Discard the bay leaf and the sprigs of thyme.

Remove the ham bones from the soup and cool slightly. Remove the meat from the bone, discard the bones and chop the meat. Return the ham to the soup and reheat. Season to taste with freshly ground pepper and lemon juice, if desired.

Serves 6–8

Note: For a finer texture, the soup can be cooled and processed before returning the meat to the pan.
Variation: For a more hearty dish, heat sliced frankfurters or spicy smoked sausage in the cooked soup.

Chicken and galangal soup

5 cm x 2 cm piece fresh galangal,
  peeled and cut into thin slices
2 cups (500 ml) coconut milk
1 cup (250 ml) chicken stock
4 fresh kaffir lime leaves, torn
1 tablespoon finely chopped fresh
  coriander roots
500 g chicken breast fillets, cut into
  thin strips
1–2 teaspoons finely chopped fresh
  red chillies
2 tablespoons fish sauce
1½ tablespoons lime juice
3 teaspoons palm sugar or soft
  brown sugar
4 tablespoons fresh coriander leaves

Place the galangal in a saucepan
with the coconut milk, stock, lime
leaves and coriander roots. Bring
to the boil, reduce the heat to
low and simmer for 10 minutes,
stirring occasionally.

Add the chicken and chilli to the
pan and simmer for 8 minutes.

Stir in the fish sauce, lime juice and
palm sugar and cook for 1 minute.
Stir in the coriander leaves. Serve
immediately garnished with extra
coriander, if desired.

Serves 4

Lentil and silverbeet soup

Chicken stock
1 kg chicken trimmings (necks, ribs,
    wings), fat removed
1 small onion, roughly chopped
1 bay leaf
3–4 sprigs fresh flat-leaf parsley
1–2 sprigs fresh oregano or thyme

1½ cups (280 g) brown lentils,
    washed
850 g silverbeet
¼ cup (60 ml) olive oil
1 large onion, finely chopped
4 cloves garlic, crushed
½ cup (25 g) finely chopped fresh
    coriander leaves
⅓ cup (80 ml) lemon juice
lemon wedges, to serve

To make the stock, place all the ingredients in a large saucepan, add 3 litres water and bring to the boil. Skim any scum from the surface. Reduce the heat and simmer for 2 hours. Strain the stock, discarding the trimmings, onion and herbs. Chill overnight. (You will need 1 litre.)

Skim any fat from the stock. Place the lentils in a large saucepan, add the stock and 1 litre water. Bring to the boil, then reduce the heat and simmer, covered, for 1 hour.

Meanwhile, remove the stems from the silverbeet and shred the leaves. Heat the oil in a saucepan over medium heat and cook the onion for 2–3 minutes, or until transparent. Add the garlic and cook for 1 minute. Add the silverbeet and toss for 2–3 minutes, or until wilted. Stir the mixture into the lentils. Add the coriander and lemon juice, season, and simmer, covered, for 15–20 minutes. Serve with the lemon wedges.

Serves 6

Pork and glass noodle soup

150 g cellophane noodles
2 teaspoons peanut oil
2 teaspoons grated fresh ginger
1.25 litres chicken stock
1/3 cup (80 ml) Chinese rice wine
1 tablespoon hoisin sauce
1 tablespoon soy sauce
4 spring onions, thinly sliced on the
    diagonal, plus extra, to garnish
300 g sliced Chinese roast pork

Soak the noodles in a large bowl
with enough boiling water to cover
for 3–4 minutes. Drain.

Heat the oil in a large saucepan.
Add the ginger and stir-fry for
1 minute. Add the stock, Chinese
rice wine, hoisin and soy sauces
and simmer for 10 minutes. Add
the spring onion and roast pork,
then cook for a further 5 minutes.

Divide the noodles among four large
bowls. Ladle in the soup and arrange
the pork on top. Garnish with extra
spring onion.

Serves 4

Cauliflower soup with smoked salmon croutons

Croutons
1 loaf day-old white bread, sliced
  lengthways
2 tablespoons butter, melted
1 clove garlic, crushed
150 g smoked salmon or gravlax
1 tablespoon finely chopped fresh dill

Soup
1 tablespoon oil
1 leek, white part only, chopped
1 clove garlic, chopped
400 g cauliflower, cut into florets
1 potato, chopped
1 cup (250 ml) chicken stock
1 cup (250 ml) milk
1¼ cups (315 ml) cream
1 tablespoon lemon juice
1 tablespoon horseradish cream
1 tablespoon snipped fresh chives

Preheat the oven to slow 150°C (300°F/Gas 2). Brush three slices of the bread on both sides with the combined butter and garlic, then season with salt. Cut off the crusts, cut each slice into four strips, then transfer the strips to a baking tray, spacing them a little apart. Bake for 30 minutes, or until crisp and golden.

Meanwhile, heat the oil in a large saucepan, add the leek and garlic, and cook over medium heat for 6–8 minutes, or until the leek is soft but not brown. Increase the heat to high, add the cauliflower, potato, stock and milk, and bring just to the boil. Reduce the heat and simmer, covered, for 20 minutes, or until the potato and cauliflower have softened.

Cool the mixture slightly, then transfer to a blender or food processor and purée until smooth. Return to a clean saucepan and add the cream, lemon and horseradish. Reheat gently for 5 minutes, then add the chives.

Cut the salmon into strips the same width as the croutons and lay along the top of each crouton. Sprinkle with the dill. Serve the soup in deep bowls with two long croutons for each person.

Serves 4 as an entrée

Curried chicken noodle soup

175 g dried thin egg noodles
2 tablespoons peanut oil
2 chicken breasts (about 250 g each)
1 onion, sliced
1 small fresh red chilli, seeded and
finely chopped
1 tablespoon finely chopped fresh
ginger
2 tablespoons Indian curry powder
3 cups (750 ml) chicken stock
800 ml coconut milk
300 g baby bok choy, cut into long
strips
1/3 cup (20 g) fresh basil, torn

Cook the noodles in a large saucepan of boiling water for 3–4 minutes, or until cooked. Drain well and set aside. Wipe the saucepan clean and dry.

Heat the oil in the dry pan and add the chicken. Cook on each side for 5 minutes, or until cooked through. Remove the chicken and keep warm.

Place the onion in the pan and cook over low heat for 8 minutes, or until softened but not browned. Add the chilli, ginger and curry powder and cook for a further 2 minutes. Add the chicken stock and bring to the boil. Reduce the heat and simmer for 20 minutes. Thinly slice the chicken on the diagonal.

Add the coconut milk to the saucepan and simmer for 10 minutes. Add the bok choy and cook for 3 minutes, then stir in the basil.

To serve, divide the noodles among four deep serving bowls. Top with slices of chicken and ladle in the soup. Serve immediately.

Serves 4

Seafood soup with rouille

Rouille
1 cooked russet potato, peeled
  and diced
1 red capsicum, grilled and peeled
2 cloves garlic, chopped
1 egg yolk
½ cup (125 ml) olive oil

1 litre fish stock
½ teaspoon saffron threads
4 sprigs fresh thyme
5 cm piece orange peel
1 small baguette
olive oil, for brushing
300 g salmon fillet, cut into 4 pieces
300 g ling fillet, cut into 4 pieces
1 calamari tube, cleaned and cut
  into rings
8 raw king prawns, shelled and
  deveined

To make the rouille, place the potato, capsicum, garlic and egg yolk in a food processor, and process until smooth. With the motor running, gradually add the olive oil until the mixture has the consistency of mayonnaise.

Preheat the oven to moderate 180°C (350°F/Gas 4). Place the stock in a large saucepan and bring to the boil. Add the saffron, thyme and orange peel. Turn off the heat and leave to stand for 10 minutes to allow the flavours to infuse.

Meanwhile, cut the baguette into 1 cm slices, brush with oil and place on a baking tray. Bake for 10 minutes, or until crisp and golden.

Strain the stock and return to the boil, then add the salmon, ling, calamari rings and prawns. Remove the stock from the heat and leave for 2 minutes, or until the seafood is cooked. Divide among four warm soup bowls and serve with the rouille and croutons.

Serves 4

Ramen noodle soup with roast pork and greens

15 g dried shiitake mushrooms
350 g Chinese broccoli, trimmed
and cut into 4 cm lengths
375 g fresh ramen noodles
1.5 litres chicken stock
3 tablespoons soy sauce
1 teaspoon sugar
350 g Chinese roast pork, thinly
sliced
1 small fresh red chilli, seeded and
thinly sliced

Soak the mushrooms in ½ cup (125 ml) hot water until softened. Squeeze the mushrooms dry, reserving the liquid. Discard the hard stalks, and finely slice the caps.

Blanch the broccoli in a large saucepan of boiling salted water for 3 minutes, or until tender but firm to the bite. Drain, then refresh in cold water.

Cook the noodles in a large saucepan of boiling water for 3 minutes, or until just softened. Drain, rinse under cold water, then set aside.

Place the stock in a large saucepan and bring to the boil. Add the sliced mushrooms and reserved mushroom liquid, soy sauce and sugar. Simmer for 2 minutes, then add the broccoli.

Divide the noodles among four large bowls. Ladle on the hot stock and vegetables. Top with the pork and sliced chilli. Serve hot.

Serves 4

Salads

Fresh tuna Niçoise

4 eggs
600 g waxy potatoes, such as kipfler
  or pink fir apple, peeled
200 g green beans
700 g tuna steaks, cut to 2 cm thick
90 ml olive oil
2 tablespoons red wine vinegar
2 tablespoons chopped fresh flat-leaf
  parsley
20 cherry tomatoes, halved
1 small red onion, thinly sliced
3/4 cup (100 g) pitted black olives

Place the eggs in a saucepan of cold water, bring to the boil, then reduce the heat and simmer for 4 minutes. Cool the eggs under cold running water, then shell and quarter.

Return the water to the boil, add the potatoes, then reduce the heat and simmer for 12 minutes, or until tender. Remove. Add the beans to the pan and cook for 3–4 minutes, or until tender but still bright green. Drain, refresh under cold water and cut in half. Slice the potatoes thickly.

Rub pepper on both sides of the tuna. Sear on a chargrill, barbecue, or in a frying pan, for 2 minutes on each side for rare, or until still pink in the middle. Cool slightly, then slice.

Combine the oil, vinegar and parsley in a small jug. Gently toss the potato, beans, tomatoes, onion and olives in a bowl, and season. Add three-quarters of the dressing and toss well. Divide among four bowls, top with the tuna and egg, and drizzle with the remaining dressing.

Serves 4

Orange sweet potato and fried noodle salad

1.25 kg orange sweet potato, peeled
  and cut into 2 cm chunks
2 tablespoons light oil
200 g roasted unsalted cashews
1 cup (50 g) finely chopped fresh
  coriander leaves
100 g packet fried noodles

Dressing
3/4 teaspoon red curry paste
90 ml coconut milk
2 tablespoons lime juice
1 1/2 tablespoons soft brown sugar
2 tablespoons light oil
4 cloves garlic, finely chopped
1 tablespoon finely chopped fresh
  ginger

Preheat the oven to moderately hot 200°C (400°F/Gas 6). Place the sweet potato and oil in a bowl, and season lightly with salt and pepper. Toss together until well coated. Place on a baking tray and bake for 30 minutes, or until tender. Drain on crumpled paper towels.

To make the dressing, combine the curry paste, coconut milk, lime juice and sugar in a food processor.

Heat the oil in a small frying pan. Add the garlic and ginger and cook over low heat for 1–2 minutes, or until light brown. Remove and add to the dressing.

Place the sweet potato, cashews, coriander, dressing and the noodles in a large bowl and toss gently until combined. Serve immediately.

Serves 4–6

Note: This is best assembled just before serving to prevent the noodles from becoming soggy.

Salmon and potato salad

800 g salmon fillet
800 g small pontiac potatoes,
  halved or quartered
3 tablespoons sour cream
1 tablespoon lemon juice
3 tablespoons good-quality
  whole-egg mayonnaise
1 teaspoon Dijon mustard
1 1/2 tablespoons horseradish
  cream
2 tablespoons finely chopped
  fresh dill
1/2 red onion, finely diced
oil, for brushing
8 cos lettuce leaves
lemon wedges, to serve

Remove any bones from the salmon, then cut into 2 cm slices. Refrigerate. Boil the potato for 20 minutes, or until tender. Drain and cool.

Combine the sour cream, lemon juice, mayonnaise, mustard and horseradish cream. Place the potato, dill and onion in a large bowl. Season, add the dressing and toss to combine.

Heat a frying pan or chargrill over high heat, brush with oil, and cook the salmon fillet for 1–2 minutes on each side. Remove from the pan.

Place two lettuce leaves in each of four serving bowls, spoon on the potato and arrange the salmon slices over the top. Top with lemon wedges and ground black pepper.

Serves 4

Fattoush

2 pitta bread rounds (17 cm diameter)
6 cos lettuce leaves, shredded
1 large Lebanese cucumber, cubed
4 tomatoes, cut into 1 cm cubes
8 spring onions, chopped
4 tablespoons finely chopped fresh
  flat-leaf parsley
1 tablespoon finely chopped fresh
  mint
2 tablespoons finely chopped fresh
  coriander

Dressing
2 cloves garlic, crushed
100 ml extra virgin olive oil
100 ml lemon juice

Preheat the oven to moderate 180°C (350°F/Gas 4). Split the bread in half through the centre and bake on a baking tray for 8–10 minutes, or until golden and crisp, turning halfway through. Break into pieces.

To make the dressing, whisk all the ingredients together in a bowl until well combined.

Place the bread and remaining salad ingredients in a serving bowl and toss to combine. Drizzle with the dressing and toss well. Season to taste with salt and freshly ground black pepper. Serve immediately.

Serves 6

Note: This is a popular Middle Eastern peasant salad which is served as an appetiser or to accompany a light meal.

Vietnamese chicken salad

400 g chicken breast fillets
1 stem lemon grass, white part only,
   finely chopped
1 tablespoon fish sauce
2 teaspoons sugar
2 tablespoons lime juice
1 1/2 tablespoons sweet chilli sauce
200 g Chinese cabbage (wom buk),
   thinly sliced
1 carrot, cut into ribbons with a
   vegetable peeler
1/2 small red onion, sliced
1/2 cup (15 g) fresh coriander leaves
1/2 cup (25 g) roughly chopped fresh
   mint
2 tablespoons fresh coriander leaves,
   extra
2 tablespoons chopped peanuts
1 tablespoon crisp fried shallots

Place the chicken and lemon grass
in a deep frying pan of lightly salted
water. Bring to the boil, then reduce
the heat and simmer gently for
8–10 minutes, or until the chicken
is just cooked through. Drain and
keep warm.

Place the fish sauce, sugar, lime
juice and sweet chilli sauce in a small
saucepan and stir over medium heat
for 1 minute, or until the sugar has
dissolved. Remove from the heat.

Place the cabbage, carrot, onion,
coriander and mint in a large bowl,
and toss together well. Drizzle over
three-quarters of the warmed
dressing, toss to combine and
transfer to a serving platter.

Slice the chicken thinly on the
diagonal, arrange over the top
of the salad and drizzle with the
remaining dressing. Garnish with
the extra coriander leaves, chopped
peanuts and crisp fried shallots.
Serve immediately.

Serves 4

Variation: Instead of Chinese
cabbage, a large green pawpaw
may be used. Remove the skin
and finely shred the fruit.

Squid salad

Dressing
2 large cloves garlic, crushed
2 teaspoons grated fresh ginger
3 small fresh red chillies, seeded
   and thinly sliced
2 tablespoons grated palm sugar
   or soft brown sugar
2 tablespoons fish sauce
2 tablespoons lime juice
½ teaspoon sesame oil

500 g squid tubes, cleaned
6 fresh kaffir lime leaves
1 stem lemon grass, white part only,
   chopped
3–4 red Asian shallots, thinly sliced
1 Lebanese cucumber, cut in half
   lengthways and thinly sliced
3 tablespoons chopped fresh
   coriander leaves
⅓ cup (8 g) fresh mint
150 g oakleaf or coral lettuce,
   leaves separated
fried red Asian shallot flakes,
   to garnish

To make the dressing, place the garlic, ginger, chilli, palm sugar, fish sauce, lime juice, sesame oil and 1 tablespoon water in a small saucepan. Stir occasionally over low heat until the sugar has dissolved. Set aside.

Cut the squid in half lengthways. Clean and remove any quills. Score a criss-cross pattern on the inside of the squid, taking care not to cut all the way through. Cut the squid into 3 cm pieces.

Place the kaffir lime leaves, lemon grass and 1.25 litres water in a saucepan and bring to the boil. Reduce the heat and simmer for 5 minutes. Add half the squid pieces and cook for 30 seconds, or until they begin to curl up and turn opaque. Remove with a slotted spoon and keep warm. Repeat with the remaining squid. Discard the lime leaves, lemon grass and liquid.

Place the squid, shallots, cucumber, coriander, mint, lettuce and dressing in a large bowl and toss together. Serve garnished with the shallot flakes.

Serves 4

Green pawpaw salad

370 g green pawpaw, peeled and
  seeded
90 g snake beans, cut into 2 cm
  lengths
2 cloves garlic
2 small fresh red chillies, chopped
5 teaspoons dried shrimp
8 cherry tomatoes, halved
50 g fresh coriander sprigs
¼ cup (40 g) chopped roasted
  peanuts

Dressing
3 tablespoons fish sauce
2 tablespoons tamarind purée
1 tablespoon lime juice
3 tablespoons grated palm sugar
  or soft brown sugar

Grate the pawpaw, sprinkle with salt
and stand for 30 minutes. Rinse well.

Cook the beans in boiling water for
3 minutes, or until tender. Plunge
into cold water, then drain.

To make the dressing, combine the
fish sauce, tamarind purée, lime juice
and palm sugar in a small bowl.

Pound the garlic and chilli in a mortar
and pestle until fine. Add the dried
shrimp and pound until puréed. Add
the pawpaw and snake beans and
lightly pound for 1 minute. Add the
tomato and pound briefly to bruise.

Combine the coriander with the
pawpaw mixture and spoon onto
serving plates. Pour the dressing
over the top. Sprinkle with the
peanuts and, if desired, sliced
red chilli.

Serves 6

Fresh beetroot and goat's cheese salad

1 kg (4 bulbs with leaves) fresh
   beetroot
200 g green beans
1 tablespoon red wine vinegar
2 tablespoons extra virgin olive oil
1 clove garlic, crushed
1 tablespoon drained capers,
   coarsely chopped
100 g goat's cheese

Trim the leaves from the beetroot. Scrub the bulbs and wash the leaves well. Add the whole bulbs to a large saucepan of boiling water, reduce the heat and simmer, covered, for 30 minutes, or until tender when pierced with the point of a knife. (The cooking time may vary depending on the size of the bulbs.)

Meanwhile, bring a saucepan of water to the boil, add the beans and cook for 3 minutes, or until just tender. Remove with a slotted spoon and plunge into a bowl of cold water. Drain well. Add the beetroot leaves to the same saucepan of boiling water and cook for 3–5 minutes, or until the leaves and stems are tender. Drain, plunge into a bowl of cold water, then drain again well. Drain and cool the beetroots, then peel the skins off and cut the bulbs into thin wedges.

To make the dressing, put the red wine vinegar, oil, garlic, capers, $1/2$ teaspoon salt and $1/2$ teaspoon pepper in a screw-top jar and shake.

To serve, divide the beans, beetroot leaves and bulbs among four serving plates. Crumble goat's cheese over the top and drizzle with the dressing.

Serves 4

Crab and spinach soba noodle salad

¼ cup (60 ml) Japanese rice vinegar
½ cup (125 ml) mirin
2 tablespoons soy sauce
1 teaspoon finely chopped fresh
  ginger
400 g English spinach
250 g fresh cooked crab meat
250 g soba noodles
2 teaspoons sesame oil
2 spring onions, finely chopped
1 sheet nori, cut into matchstick-
  sized strips

Combine the rice vinegar, mirin, soy sauce and ginger in a small bowl. Set aside.

Bring a large saucepan of salted water to the boil. Blanch the spinach for 15–20 seconds, then remove with a slotted spoon (reserve the water in the pan). Place the spinach in a bowl of ice-cold water for 30 seconds. Drain and squeeze out the moisture, then coarsely chop. Combine with the crab meat and 2 tablespoons of the rice vinegar mixture.

Bring the pan of water back to the boil and cook the noodles for 5 minutes, or until just tender. Drain, then rinse under cold water. Toss with the sesame oil, spring onion and the remaining dressing. Divide the noodles among individual bowls, top with the spinach and crab meat and scatter with nori.

Serves 4

Prawn and saffron potato salad

16 raw medium prawns
1/3 cup (80 ml) olive oil
450 g new potatoes, cut in half
1/4 teaspoon saffron threads, crushed
1 clove garlic, crushed
1 birds eye chilli, seeded and finely
  chopped
1 teaspoon grated lime rind
1/4 cup (60 ml) lime juice
200 g baby rocket

Preheat the oven to moderate 180°C (350°F/Gas 4). Peel and devein the prawns, leaving the tails intact.

Heat 2 tablespoons of the oil in a frying pan and brown the potatoes. Transfer to a roasting tin and toss gently with the saffron and some salt and black pepper. Bake for 25 minutes, or until tender.

Heat a chargrill pan over medium heat. Toss the prawns in a small bowl with the garlic, chilli, lime rind and 1 tablespoon of the oil. Grill the prawns for 2 minutes each side, or until pink and cooked.

In a small jar, shake up the lime juice and the remaining oil. Season with salt and pepper. Place the potatoes on a plate, top with the rocket and prawns and drizzle with dressing.

Serves 4

Roasted fennel and orange salad

8 baby fennel bulbs
100 ml olive oil
1 teaspoon sea salt
2 oranges
1 tablespoon lemon juice
1 red onion, halved and thinly sliced
100 g Kalamata olives
2 tablespoons chopped fresh mint
1 tablespoon roughly chopped fresh
flat-leaf parsley

Preheat the oven to moderately hot 200°C (400°F/Gas 6). Trim and reserve the fennel fronds. Remove the stalks and cut a 5 mm slice off the base of each fennel. Cut each bulb into 6 wedges. Place in an ovenproof dish and drizzle with ¼ cup (60 ml) oil. Add the salt and plenty of pepper. Bake for 40–60 minutes, or until the fennel is tender and slightly caramelised. Cool.

Cut a slice off the top and bottom of each orange. Using a small, sharp knife, carefully remove the skin and as much pith as possible. Working over a bowl, cut down each side of a segment between the flesh and the membrane, and lift the segment out. Repeat with all the segments. Squeeze out any remaining juice from the membrane.

Whisk the remaining olive oil into the orange and lemon juice until emulsified. Season. Combine the orange segments, onion and olives, pour on half the dressing and mix in half the mint. Transfer to a serving dish and top with the roasted fennel. Drizzle with the remaining dressing, and scatter with the parsley and the remaining mint. Roughly chop the fronds and scatter over the salad.

Serves 4

Pork, prawn and vermicelli salad in lettuce cups

vegetable oil, for frying
100 g dried rice vermicelli
3 tablespoons peanut oil
1 clove garlic, crushed
1 tablespoon finely chopped fresh
  ginger
3 spring onions, finely sliced and
  green ends reserved for garnish
150 g pork mince
500 g raw prawns, peeled, deveined
  and roughly chopped
2 tablespoons Chinese rice wine
2 tablespoons soy sauce
2 tablespoons hoisin sauce
1 tablespoon brown bean sauce
1/2 teaspoon sugar
1/4 cup (60 ml) chicken stock
12 iceberg lettuce leaves, trimmed
  into cups

Fill a deep, heavy-based saucepan one-third full of oil and heat to 170°C (325°F), or until a cube of bread browns in 20 seconds. Add the vermicelli in batches and deep-fry until puffed up but not browned — this will only take a few seconds. Remove with a slotted spoon and drain on crumpled paper towels.

Heat the peanut oil in a wok over high heat and swirl to coat the side. Add the garlic, ginger and spring onion, and stir-fry for 1 minute, being careful not to burn the garlic.

Add the pork mince to the wok, breaking up the lumps, and cook for a further 4 minutes. Add the prawns and stir-fry for 2 minutes, or until they begin to change colour.

Add the Chinese rice wine, soy sauce, hoisin sauce, brown bean sauce, sugar, chicken stock and 1/2 teaspoon salt and stir until combined. Cook over high heat for 2 minutes, or until the mixture thickens slightly. Divide the noodles among the lettuce cups, top with the pork and prawn mixture and garnish with the reserved spring onion. Serve immediately.

Serves 6

Chickpea and flat bread salad

3 pieces Lebanese bread
6 firm, ripe tomatoes, chopped
1½ red capsicums, seeded and
    sliced
9 spring onions, sliced
600 g canned chickpeas, rinsed
    and drained
½ cup (125 ml) olive oil
2 teaspoons grated lemon rind
¼ cup (60 ml) lemon juice
1½ teaspoons ground cumin
4 tablespoons chopped fresh
    flat-leaf parsley

Preheat the oven to moderately hot 200°C (400°F/Gas 6). Place the bread on a baking tray and bake for 8 minutes, or until crisp. Cool, then break up into pieces.

Place the tomato, capsicum, spring onion, chickpeas and bread pieces in a large bowl, and toss gently. Combine the oil, lemon rind and juice and cumin, and pour over the salad. Scatter the parsley over the top, mix well and serve.

Serves 4

Note: This salad can be made in advance, but don't add the flat bread pieces until just prior to serving or they will become soggy.

Roast duck and noodle salad

400 g fresh flat Chinese egg noodles
1 teaspoon sesame oil, plus
  1 tablespoon extra
1 tablespoon grated fresh ginger
1/2–1 teaspoon sambal oelek,
  or to taste
2 tablespoons fish sauce
2 tablespoons rice wine vinegar
1 tablespoon lime juice
1/4 teaspoon Chinese five-spice
  powder
1 tablespoon soft brown sugar
2 tablespoons peanut oil
1 cup (50 g) roughly chopped fresh
  coriander, plus extra leaves, to
  garnish
1 Chinese roast duck, meat removed
  from bones and sliced into bite-size
  pieces
2 cups (180 g) bean sprouts
3 spring onions, thinly sliced
1/2 cup (80 g) roasted peanuts,
  chopped

Bring a large saucepan of lightly salted water to the boil. Add the noodles and cook for 3–4 minutes, or until just tender. Rinse under cold water, drain and toss with 1 teaspoon sesame oil.

Place the ginger, sambal oelek, fish sauce, vinegar, lime juice, five-spice and sugar in a small bowl and stir to dissolve the sugar. Whisk in the extra sesame oil and the peanut oil, then stir in the coriander. Season to taste with salt.

Place the noodles, duck, bean sprouts and spring onion in a large bowl. Pour on the dressing and toss to coat. Season to taste. Garnish with the chopped peanuts and extra coriander leaves.

Serves 4

Smoked trout Caesar salad

350 g skinless smoked trout fillets
300 g green beans, halved
6 tinned artichokes, drained, rinsed
  and quartered
2 eggs
1 small clove garlic, chopped
2 teaspoons Dijon mustard
2 tablespoons white wine vinegar
1/3 cup (80 ml) olive oil
6 slices (200 g) day-old Italian-style
  bread (ciabatta), cut into 2 cm
  cubes
2 tablespoons capers, drained
1 baby cos lettuce, leaves separated
1/2 cup (40 g) freshly shaved
  Parmesan

Flake the trout into 4 cm shards and place in a bowl. Cook the beans in boiling water for 3 minutes, or until tender and still bright green. Refresh under cold water. Add to the bowl, with the artichoke.

Poach the eggs in simmering water for 40 seconds, or until just cooked. Place in a food processor with the garlic, mustard and vinegar, and process until smooth. With the motor running, add 2 tablespoons oil in a thin stream, processing until thick and creamy. Season to taste.

Heat the remaining oil in a frying pan, add the bread and capers, and cook over high heat for 3–5 minutes, or until golden. Line four bowls with the cos leaves. Divide the trout mixture among the bowls, drizzle with the dressing and top with the croutons, capers and Parmesan.

Serves 4

Prawn salad with Asian dressing

Dressing
1/3 cup (80 ml) rice vinegar (see Note)
1/4 cup (60 ml) soy sauce
2 tablespoons honey
1 teaspoon sesame oil
1–2 teaspoons grated fresh ginger
2 cloves garlic, crushed

2 carrots (150 g), cut into thin 5 cm long strips
1 red capsicum, thinly sliced
1/2 daikon radish (75 g), peeled and cut into thin 5 cm long strips
10 g garlic chives, cut into 5 cm lengths
750 g cooked medium prawns, peeled and deveined, with tails intact
200 g baby English spinach leaves

Place all the dressing ingredients in a small saucepan and warm over medium heat for 2–3 minutes, or until the honey dissolves; do not boil. Remove the pan from the heat.

Place the thin strips of carrot, capsicum, radish and garlic chives in a bowl and toss with tongs to evenly distribute. Add the prawns to the vegetables, pour on half the dressing, then toss thoroughly again.

To assemble the salad, make a bed of spinach on four plates (or a platter), place the mixed vegetable strips and prawns on the spinach and drizzle with the remaining dressing. Serve immediately.

Serves 4

Note: Rice vinegar is a pale yellow sweet-tasting vinegar made from rice. There aren't really any suitable substitutes.

Pork and udon noodle salad with lime dressing

Dressing
⅓ cup (80 ml) lime juice
1 tablespoon sesame oil
2 tablespoons ponzu
¼ cup (90 g) honey

400 g fresh udon noodles
500 g pork fillet
1 tablespoon sesame oil
200 g roasted unsalted peanuts
2 large fresh red chillies, seeded
  and finely diced
2 teaspoons finely chopped fresh
  ginger
1 large cucumber, peeled, halved,
  seeds removed and julienned
200 g bean sprouts
½ cup (25 g) chopped fresh
  coriander leaves

Preheat the oven to moderately hot 200°C (400°F/Gas 6). To make the dressing, place the lime juice, sesame oil, ponzu and honey in a screwtop jar and shake.

Cook the noodles in a saucepan of boiling water for 1–2 minutes, or until tender. Drain, rinse and set aside.

Trim the fat and sinew off the pork and brush with the sesame oil. Season. Heat a non-stick frying pan until very hot and cook the pork for 5–6 minutes, or until browned on all sides and cooked to your liking. Remove from the pan and rest for 5 minutes.

Combine the noodles, peanuts, chilli, ginger, cucumber, bean sprouts and coriander and toss well. Cut the pork into thin slices, add to the salad with the dressing and toss before serving.

Serves 4

Tuna, tomato and rocket pasta salad

350 g dried fettucine
350 g tuna steaks
1/2 cup (75 g) sun-dried tomatoes, drained, roughly chopped, reserving 2 tablespoons oil
2 cloves garlic, crushed
1/2 cup (115 g) sun-dried capsicums, drained and roughly chopped
100 g capers, drained
1 cup (175 g) black olives, pitted and quartered
100 g baby rocket leaves

Bring a large saucepan of lightly salted water to the boil. Add the pasta and cook until *al dente*. Drain. Meanwhile, lightly brush a chargrill plate with oil and cook the tuna for 1–2 minutes each side (it should be rare in the centre), or until cooked to your liking. Cut the tuna into 2.5 cm cubes. Keep warm.

Heat the reserved sun-dried tomato oil in a saucepan over medium heat. Add the tomato, garlic, capsicum, capers and olives, and cook, stirring, for 5–6 minutes, or until the mixture is heated through.

Place the pasta, tomato mixture and rocket in a large bowl, season and toss to combine. Divide among four serving plates and top with the tuna. Serve with lemon wedges and shaved Parmesan, if desired.

Serves 4

Note: If you prefer the tuna rare, use very fresh sashimi tuna.
If baby rocket leaves are not available, use larger rocket leaves and tear them into pieces.

Lamb and rice noodle salad with peanut dressing

500 g lamb fillet, cut lengthways
  into thin strips
2 tablespoons light soy sauce
1 tablespoon rice wine
125 g dried rice noodle sticks
1 telegraph cucumber, unpeeled, cut
  into long thin strips with a vegetable
  peeler
100 g chopped unsalted toasted
  peanuts
fresh coriander sprigs, to garnish

Spicy peanut dressing
3 cloves garlic
175 g smooth peanut butter
4 tablespoons soy sauce
1 cup (30 g) fresh coriander leaves
1 tablespoon rice wine vinegar
1 tablespoon Chinese rice wine
  or dry sherry
2 tablespoons palm sugar or soft
  brown sugar
1 small fresh red chilli, roughly
  chopped

Combine the lamb, soy sauce
and rice wine in a bowl. Cover
and marinate for 1 hour.

To make the peanut dressing, purée
all the ingredients with 2 tablespoons
water in a blender until smooth.

Soak the noodles in a bowl of boiling
water for 15 minutes. Drain, then
rinse under cold water.

Heat a chargrill or grill until very hot
and sear the lamb slices in batches
for 30 seconds on each side, or until
cooked to your liking, then transfer
to a large bowl. Add the noodles,
cucumber and three-quarters of
the dressing and toss to combine.
Serve on a dish and drizzle with the
remaining dressing. Scatter with the
peanuts and garnish with the
coriander sprigs.

Serves 4

Chargrilled baby octopus salad

1 kg baby octopus
1 teaspoon sesame oil
2 tablespoons lime juice
2 tablespoons fish sauce
¼ cup (60 ml) sweet chilli sauce
200 g mixed salad leaves
1 red capsicum, very thinly sliced
2 small Lebanese cucumbers, seeded
  and cut into ribbons
4 red Asian shallots, chopped
100 g toasted unsalted peanuts,
  chopped

To clean the octopus, remove the head from the tentacles by cutting just underneath the eyes. To clean the head, carefully slit the head open and remove the gut. Cut it in half. Push out the beak from the centre of the tentacles, then cut the tentacles into sets of four or two, depending on their size. Pull the skin away from the head and tentacles if it comes away easily. The eyes will come off as you pull off the skin.

To make the marinade, combine the sesame oil, lime juice, fish sauce and chilli sauce in a shallow, non-metallic bowl. Add the octopus, and stir to coat. Cover and chill for 2 hours.

Heat a chargrill pan or barbecue to very hot. Drain the octopus, reserving the marinade, then cook in batches for 3–5 minutes, turning occasionally.

Pour the reserved marinade into a small saucepan, bring to the boil and cook for 2 minutes, or until it has slightly thickened.

Divide the salad leaves among four plates, scatter with capsicum and cucumber, then top with the octopus. Drizzle with the marinade and top with the Asian shallots and peanuts.

Serves 4 as an entrée

Prawn, prosciutto and rocket salad

4 Roma tomatoes, quartered
  lengthways
1 clove garlic, chopped
⅓ cup (80 ml) olive oil
8 slices prosciutto
20 raw medium prawns, peeled,
  deveined and cut in half lengthways
2 teaspoons balsamic vinegar
2 avocados, stone removed and
  thinly sliced
60 g baby rocket leaves

Preheat the oven to very slow 140°C (275°F/Gas 1). Place the tomato quarters in a bowl and toss with the garlic, 1 tablespoon of the oil and some salt and pepper. Place the tomato quarters on a baking tray and roast for 1½ hours. Remove from the oven.

Lightly brush the prosciutto with a little of the remaining olive oil. Heat a non-stick frying pan over medium–high heat. When hot, add the prosciutto in two batches, cooking for 3–4 minutes each side until it starts to become crisp. Drain on paper towels to remove any excess oil, then break into shards.

Heat a chargrill pan until it is hot, lightly oil the pan, then cook the prawns in two batches for 2 minutes each side. Season well and transfer to a large serving bowl.

Combine the rest of the olive oil with the balsamic vinegar. To assemble the salad, place the tomato, prosciutto, avocado and rocket in the bowl with the prawns. Drizzle with 1 tablespoon of the dressing, then gently toss together. Drizzle with the remaining dressing and serve.

Serves 4

Thai beef salad

500 g rump steak
3½ tablespoons lime juice
2 tablespoons fish sauce
1 teaspoon grated palm sugar
2 cloves garlic, crushed
1 stem lemon grass, white part
  only, finely sliced
2 small fresh red chillies, finely sliced
4 red Asian shallots, finely sliced
15–20 fresh mint leaves
½ cup (15 g) fresh coriander leaves
125 g cherry tomatoes, halved
1 Lebanese cucumber, halved
  lengthwise and thinly sliced
3 cups (180 g) shredded Chinese
  cabbage
¼ cup (20 g) prepared Asian
  fried onions
1 tablespoon prepared Asian
  fried garlic
¼ cup (40 g) crushed peanuts,
  to garnish

Heat a non-stick frying pan over
medium–high heat until very hot.
Cook the steak for 4 minutes each
side, then remove and cool.

Combine the lime juice, fish sauce,
palm sugar, garlic, lemon grass and
chilli and stir to dissolve the sugar.
Add the shallots, mint and coriander.
Thinly slice the beef across the grain,
and toss through the mixture. Chill
for 15 minutes. Add the tomato and
cucumber and toss well. Arrange the
cabbage on a serving platter and top
with the beef mixture. Sprinkle with
the fried onion, garlic and peanuts.

Serves 4

Greek salad

4 tomatoes, cut into wedges
1 telegraph cucumber, peeled,
    halved, seeded and cut into
    small cubes
2 green capsicums, seeded, halved
    lengthways and cut into strips
1 red onion, finely sliced
16 Kalamata olives
250 g good-quality firm feta,
    cut into cubes
3 tablespoons fresh flat-leaf parsley
12 whole fresh mint leaves
½ cup (125 ml) good-quality olive oil
2 tablespoons lemon juice
1 clove garlic, crushed

Place the tomato, cucumber, capsicum, onion, olives, feta and half the parsley and mint leaves in a large salad bowl, and gently mix together.

Place the oil, juice and garlic in a screwtop jar, season and shake until combined. Pour the dressing over the salad and toss lightly. Garnish with the remaining parsley and mint.

Serves 4

Asian salmon and noodle salad

½ cup (125 ml) lime juice
2 tablespoons grated fresh ginger
500 g fresh salmon fillet, skinned,
   bones removed, thinly sliced
600 g fresh egg noodles
2 tablespoons mirin
2 tablespoons fish sauce
2 teaspoons grated palm sugar
   or soft brown sugar
¼ cup (60 ml) peanut oil
2 teaspoons sesame oil
1 small fresh red chilli, chopped
8 spring onions, sliced
2 tablespoons whole fresh coriander
   leaves
1 tablespoon fresh Vietnamese mint,
   finely chopped
2 tablespoons chopped fresh garlic
   chives
fresh coriander leaves, to garnish

Combine the lime juice and ginger
in a bowl, add the salmon and toss
to coat. Refrigerate for 2 hours (but
no longer).

Cook the noodles in boiling water
for 2–3 minutes. Drain and refresh
in cold water.

Remove the fish from the marinade.
Add the mirin, fish sauce, palm sugar,
peanut and sesame oils, and chilli
to the marinade. Mix well. Place
the noodles, fish, spring onion and
fresh herbs in a large bowl, add the
dressing and toss to coat. Garnish
with the coriander leaves.

Serves 4

Pear and walnut salad with lime vinaigrette

1 small baguette, cut into
 16 thin slices
oil, for brushing
1 clove garlic, cut in half
1 cup (100 g) walnuts
200 g cheese
400 g mesclun leaves
2 pears, cut into 2 cm cubes,
 mixed with 2 tablespoons lime juice

Lime vinaigrette
3 tablespoons extra virgin olive oil
¼ cup (60 ml) lime juice
2 tablespoons raspberry vinegar

Preheat the oven to moderate 180°C (350°F/Gas 4). Brush the baguette slices with a little oil, rub with the cut side of the garlic, then place on a baking tray. Bake for 10 minutes, or until crisp and golden. Place the walnuts on a baking tray and roast for 5–8 minutes, or until just slightly browned—shake the tray to ensure even colouring. Allow to cool for 5 minutes.

To make the lime vinaigrette, whisk together the olive oil, lime juice, raspberry vinegar, 1 teaspoon salt and ½ teaspoon ground black pepper in a bowl. Set aside until ready to use.

Spread some of the cheese on each crouton, then cook under a hot grill for 2–3 minutes, or until hot.

Place the mesclun, pears and walnuts in a bowl, add the vinaigrette and toss through. Divide the salad among four serving bowls and serve with the cheese croutons.

Serves 4

Vietnamese prawn and cabbage salad

1/3 cup (80 ml) rice vinegar
2 tablespoons fish sauce
2 tablespoons lime juice
2 tablespoons grated palm sugar
  or soft brown sugar
1 small fresh red chilli, seeded
  and finely chopped
2 tablespoons peanut oil
1 clove garlic, crushed
20 raw medium prawns, peeled
  and deveined with tails intact
2 cups (150 g) thinly sliced cabbage
2 cups (150 g) thinly sliced red
  cabbage
200 g sliced drained bamboo shoots
1/2 cup (10 g) fresh mint leaves
1/2 cup (15 g) fresh coriander leaves
2 fresh long green chillies, seeded
  and thinly sliced on the diagonal
lime wedges, to serve

To make the salad dressing, combine the rice vinegar, fish sauce, lime juice, palm sugar and red chilli in a small bowl and stir together until the sugar has dissolved.

Heat the peanut oil in a non-stick frying pan or wok over medium heat. When hot, add the garlic and cook for 10 seconds, stirring constantly. Add the prawns in two batches and cook for about 2 minutes each side, or until pink and cooked through, then remove from the pan.

Place the cabbages, bamboo shoots, herbs and green chilli in a serving bowl and mix together well. Add the prawns to the bowl, drizzle the dressing over the salad, season with pepper and toss well. Serve with lime wedges.

Serves 4

Chicken Waldorf salad

3 cups (750 ml) chicken stock
2 chicken breast fillets, skin removed
2 red apples
2 green apples
2 sticks celery, sliced
100 g toasted walnuts
1/2 cup (125 g) whole-egg mayonnaise
1/4 cup (60 g) sour cream
1/2 teaspoon chopped fresh tarragon
1 baby cos lettuce

Bring the stock to the boil in a medium saucepan. Remove from the heat, add the chicken to the stock, then cover and allow to cool in the liquid for 10 minutes, by which time the chicken should be cooked. Test by touching with your finger— the chicken should feel quite springy.

Cut the apples into bite sized pieces. Shred the chicken breasts and place in a large bowl with the apple, celery, walnuts, mayonnaise, sour cream and tarragon. Season with salt and freshly ground black pepper, and toss well to combine. Separate the lettuce leaves and arrange them in a serving bowl. Pile the Waldorf salad over the lettuce and serve.

Serves 4

Pasta

Creamy chicken and peppercorn pappardelle

2 chicken breast fillets (420 g in total)
30 g butter
1 onion, halved and thinly sliced
2 tablespoons drained green
  peppercorns, slightly crushed
1/2 cup (125 ml) white wine
300 ml cream
400 g fresh pappardelle pasta
1/3 cup (80 g) sour cream (optional)
2 tablespoons chopped fresh chives

Cut the chicken in half so that you have four flat fillets and season with salt and pepper. Melt the butter in a frying pan, add the chicken and cook for 3 minutes each side, or until lightly browned and cooked through. Remove from the pan, cut into slices and keep warm.

Add the onion and peppercorns to the same pan and cook over medium heat for 3 minutes, or until the onion has softened slightly. Add the wine and cook for 1 minute, or until reduced by half. Stir in the cream and cook for 4–5 minutes, or until thickened slightly, then season with salt and black pepper. Meanwhile, cook the pasta in a large saucepan of boiling water until *al dente*, then drain. Mix together the pasta, chicken and any juices and cream sauce. Divide the pasta among serving bowls, top with a dollop of sour cream and sprinkle with chives.

Serves 4

Angel hair pasta with garlic, scallops and rocket

20 large scallops with roe
250 g angel hair pasta
150 ml extra virgin olive oil
2 cloves garlic, finely chopped
¼ cup (60 ml) white wine
1 tablespoon lemon juice
100 g baby rocket leaves
½ cup (25 g) chopped fresh
  coriander leaves

Trim any veins, membrane or hard white muscle from the scallops. Pat dry with paper towels. Bring a large saucepan of water to the boil, add the pasta and cook until *al dente*. Drain the pasta well and toss with 1 tablespoon oil.

Meanwhile, heat 1 tablespoon oil in a frying pan, add the garlic and cook for a few seconds, or until fragrant. Do not brown. Add the combined wine and lemon juice, and remove from the heat.

Heat a chargrill plate over high heat and brush with a little oil. Season the scallops with salt and pepper and cook for 1 minute each side, or until just cooked. Gently reheat the garlic mixture, add the rocket and stir over medium heat for 1–2 minutes, or until wilted. Toss through the pasta then add the remaining oil and half the coriander, and mix well. Divide the pasta among four serving bowls, arrange the scallops over the top and garnish with the remaining coriander.

Serves 4

Variation: Add ½ teaspoon dried chilli flakes just before the wine and lemon juice for an added kick.

Macaroni cheese
with pancetta

2½ cups (390 g) macaroni
75 g pancetta, diced
2 cups (500 ml) cream
1 cup (125 g) grated Cheddar
2 cups (260 g) grated Gruyère
1 cup (100 g) grated Parmesan
1 clove garlic, crushed
2 teaspoons Dijon mustard
½ teaspoon paprika
2 tablespoons snipped fresh chives
fresh chives, extra, to garnish

Bring a large saucepan of lightly salted water to the boil. Add the macaroni and cook until *al dente*. Drain, cover and keep warm.

Meanwhile, place the pancetta in a large saucepan and cook over high heat, stirring, for 4 minutes, or until well browned and slightly crisp. Drain on paper towels. Reduce the heat to medium, stir in the cream and simmer. Add the cheeses, garlic, mustard and paprika, and stir for 5 minutes, or until the cheeses have melted and the sauce has thickened. Season.

Add the macaroni and pancetta and stir for 1 minute, or until heated through. Stir in the chives, garnish with the extra chives and serve.

Serves 4

Pasta with seared prawns

8 raw jumbo prawns
2 tablespoons olive oil
100 g unsalted butter, chopped
1½ tablespoons drained baby capers
250 g angel hair pasta
¼ cup (60 ml) lemon juice
1 teaspoon grated lemon rind
1–2 small fresh red chillies, seeded
    and thinly sliced
½ cup (15 g) chopped fresh flat-leaf
    parsley
lemon wedges, to serve

Remove the heads from the prawns. Slice them down the back without cutting right through, then open them out, leaving the tails and shells intact. Rinse under cold water and pull out the vein. Pat dry, then season lightly.

Heat the oil and half the butter in a large frying pan, add the capers and cook for 1 minute. Remove from the pan and set aside. Add the prawns and cook, cut-side-down first, for 2–3 minutes each side, or until pink and cooked. Remove and keep warm.

Cook the pasta in a saucepan of boiling water until *al dente*. Drain, reserving 1–2 tablespoons of the cooking liquid.

Melt the remaining butter in the frying pan, add the lemon juice and rind, capers and chilli and stir until fragrant. Add the pasta and parsley and toss until the pasta is coated with the butter. If needed, add some of the reserved cooking liquid to moisten the pasta. Season.

Divide the pasta among serving bowls, top with the prawns and serve with lemon wedges.

Serves 2 (main) or 4 (entrée)

Peppered pork, zucchini and garganelli

450 g pork fillet
3–4 teaspoons cracked black
  peppercorns
80 g butter
250 g garganelli pasta
1 onion, halved and thinly sliced
2 large zucchini, thinly sliced
2/3 cup (20 g) fresh basil, torn
3/4 cup (155 g) baby black olives
1/2 cup (60 g) grated Romano cheese

Cut the pork fillet in half widthways and roll in the pepper and some salt. Heat half the butter in a large deep frying pan, add the pork and cook for 4 minutes on each side, or until golden brown and just cooked through. Remove from the pan and cut into 5 mm slices, then set aside and keep warm.

Cook the pasta in a large saucepan of boiling water until *al dente*; drain well and return to the pan.

Meanwhile, melt the remaining butter in the frying pan, add the onion and cook, stirring, over medium heat for about 3 minutes, or until soft. Add the zucchini and toss for 5 minutes, or until starting to soften. Add the basil, olives, sliced pork and any juices and toss well. Stir the pork mixture through the hot pasta, then season to taste with salt and cracked black pepper. Serve immediately topped with the cheese.

Serves 4

Spaghetti with olive, caper and anchovy sauce

375 g spaghetti
1/3 cup (80 ml) olive oil
2 onions, finely chopped
3 cloves garlic, finely chopped
1/2 teaspoon chilli flakes
6 large ripe tomatoes, diced
4 tablespoons capers in brine, rinsed, drained
7–8 anchovies in oil, drained, minced
150 g Kalamata olives
3 tablespoons chopped fresh flat-leaf parsley

Bring a large saucepan of salted water to the boil, add the spaghetti and cook until *al dente*. Drain.

Meanwhile, heat the oil in a large saucepan, add the onion and cook over medium heat for 5 minutes. Add the garlic and chilli flakes, and cook for 30 seconds, then add the tomato, capers and anchovies. Simmer over low heat for 5–10 minutes, or until thick and pulpy, then stir in the olives and parsley.

Stir the pasta through the sauce. Season with salt and freshly ground black pepper and serve immediately with crusty bread.

Serves 6

Creamy pasta gnocchi with peas and prosciutto

100 g thinly sliced prosciutto
3 teaspoons oil
2 eggs
1 cup (250 ml) cream
⅓ cup (35 g) finely grated Parmesan
2 tablespoons chopped fresh flat-leaf
  parsley
1 tablespoon chopped fresh chives
250 g fresh or frozen peas
500 g pasta gnocchi

Cut the prosciutto into 5 mm wide strips. Heat the oil in a frying pan over medium heat, add the prosciutto and cook for 2 minutes, or until crisp. Drain on paper towels. Place the eggs, cream, Parmesan and herbs in a bowl and whisk well.

Bring a saucepan of salted water to the boil. Add the peas and cook for 5 minutes, or until just tender. Leaving the pan on the heat, use a slotted spoon and transfer the peas to the bowl of cream mixture, and then add ¼ cup (60 ml) of the cooking liquid to the same bowl. Using a potato masher or the back of a fork, roughly mash the peas.

Add the gnocchi to the boiling water and cook until *al dente*. Drain well, then return to the pan. Add the cream mixture and warm through over low heat, gently stirring for about 30 seconds until the gnocchi is coated in the sauce. Season to taste with salt and pepper. Divide among warmed plates, top with the prosciutto and serve immediately.

Serves 4

Note: Be careful not to overheat the sauce, as the egg will begin to set and the result will look like a scrambled egg sauce.

Roast pumpkin, feta and rocket penne

1.2 kg butternut or jap pumpkin,
   peeled and cut into 2 cm cubes
1 teaspoon fresh rosemary
4 cloves garlic, crushed
2 tablespoons olive oil
500 g penne
20 g butter
1 large red onion, sliced
1 tablespoon honey
½ cup (125 ml) chicken stock
200 g feta, crumbled
100 g fresh rocket leaves
shaved Parmesan, to garnish

Preheat the oven to moderately hot 200°C (400°F/Gas 6). Place the pumpkin in a roasting tin with the rosemary, garlic and 1 tablespoon olive oil, and toss to coat. Bake for 30 minutes, or until the pumpkin is soft and golden. Season.

Meanwhile, cook the penne in a large saucepan of lightly salted boiling water until *al dente*. Drain, return to the pan and stir in the butter. Keep warm.

Heat the remaining oil in a frying pan over medium heat, add the onion and cook for 3–5 minutes, then add the honey and cook for 2 minutes, or until the onion starts to caramelise. Add the stock and simmer gently for 5–7 minutes, or until reduced slightly.

Add the roast pumpkin to the onion mixture, stir to combine, then add to the pasta with the feta and rocket. Toss to combine and season to taste. Garnish with the Parmesan.

Serves 4

Cavatelli with pecorino and a herb sauce

400 g cavatelli pasta
80 g butter
2 cloves garlic, crushed
3 tablespoons chopped fresh chives
3 tablespoons shredded fresh basil
1 tablespoon shredded fresh sage
1 teaspoon fresh thyme
1/4 cup (60 ml) warm vegetable stock
2/3 cup (60 g) firmly packed grated
  pecorino cheese (see Note)

Cook the pasta in a large saucepan of rapidly boiling water until *al dente*. Meanwhile, heat the butter in a small saucepan over medium heat, add the garlic and cook for 1 minute, or until fragrant. Add the chives, basil, sage and thyme and cook for a further minute.

Drain the pasta and return to the pan. Add the herb mixture and stock. Return to the heat for 2–3 minutes, or until warmed through. Season to taste with salt and cracked black pepper. Add the grated pecorino and stir until well combined. Divide among four warm serving bowls and garnish with sage leaves, if desired.

Serves 4

Note: Pecorino is sheep's milk cheese with a sharp flavour. If unavailable, use Parmesan instead.

Tortellini boscaiola

30 g butter
4 rashers bacon, chopped
2 cloves garlic, crushed
1 small leek, thinly sliced
300 g Swiss brown or button
  mushrooms, sliced
¼ cup (60 ml) dry white wine
1½ cups (375 ml) cream
1 teaspoon chopped fresh thyme
500 g fresh veal tortellini
½ cup (50 g) grated Parmesan
1 tablespoon chopped fresh parsley

Melt the butter in a large frying pan, add the bacon and cook over medium heat for 5 minutes, or until crisp. Add the garlic and leek, and cook for 2 minutes, then add the mushrooms and cook for 8 minutes, or until softened. Add the wine, cream and thyme, bring to the boil, then reduce the heat and simmer for 10 minutes, or until the sauce has thickened.

Meanwhile, cook the tortellini in a large saucepan of lightly salted boiling water until *al dente*. Drain. Add the Parmesan to the sauce and stir over low heat until melted. Season. Combine the sauce with the tortellini and parsley.

Serves 4–6

Cajun scallops, conchigliette and buttery corn sauce

350 g conchigliette or conchiglie
20 large scallops, without roe
2 tablespoons Cajun spice mix
2 tablespoons corn oil
250 g butter
3 cloves garlic, crushed
400 g can corn kernels, drained
1/4 cup (60 ml) lime juice
4 tablespoons finely chopped fresh
  coriander leaves

Cook the pasta in a large saucepan of boiling water until *al dente*. Drain and return to the pan to keep warm. Meanwhile, pat the scallops dry with paper towel and lightly coat in the spice mix. Heat the oil in a large frying pan and cook the scallops for 1 minute each side over high heat (ensuring they are well spaced), then remove from the pan, cover and keep warm.

Reduce the heat to medium, add the butter and cook for 4 minutes, or until foaming and golden brown. Remove from the heat, add the garlic, corn and lime juice. Gently toss the corn mixture through the pasta with 2 tablespoons of the coriander and season well. Divide among four serving plates, top with the scallops, drizzle with any juices and sprinkle with the remaining coriander.

Serves 4

Notes: Scallops should not be crowded in the pan or they will stew and become tough.
To achieve the most delicious flavours, don't use a non-stick frying pan—it will prevent the butter from properly browning and the juices from caramelising.

Rotelle with chickpeas, tomato and parsley

375 g rotelle pasta
1 tablespoon ground cumin
½ cup (125 ml) olive oil
1 red onion, halved and thinly sliced
3 cloves garlic, crushed
400 g can chickpeas, drained
3 large tomatoes, diced
½ cup (15 g) chopped fresh flat-leaf
   parsley
¼ cup (60 ml) lemon juice

Cook the pasta in a large saucepan of boiling water until *al dente*. Drain and return to the pan.

Meanwhile, heat a large frying pan over medium heat, add the cumin and cook, tossing, for 1 minute, or until fragrant. Remove from the pan. Heat half the oil in the same pan and cook the onion over medium heat for 2–3 minutes, or until soft. Stir in the garlic, chickpeas, tomato and parsley and stir until warmed through. Gently toss through the pasta.

Place the lemon juice, cumin and remaining oil in a jar with a lid and shake together well. Add the dressing to the saucepan with the pasta and chickpea mixture, return to the stove-top over low heat and stir until warmed through. Season well with salt and cracked black pepper. Serve hot with grated Parmesan, or you can serve it cold. If serving cold, rinse the pasta under cold running water before adding the chickpea mixture and do not return to the heat.

Serves 4

Spaghetti marinara

1 tablespoon olive oil
1 onion, chopped
3 cloves garlic, crushed
2 x 400 g cans crushed tomatoes
2 tablespoons tomato paste
2/3 cup (170 ml) dry white wine
2 teaspoons soft brown sugar
1 teaspoon finely grated lemon rind
2 tablespoons chopped fresh basil
12 raw medium prawns, peeled
  and deveined
12 large white scallops, without roe
2 small calamari tubes (300 g),
  cleaned and cut into 1 cm rings
300 g spaghetti
2 tablespoons finely chopped fresh
  flat-leaf parsley
shaved Parmesan, to serve

Heat the oil in a large saucepan, add the onion and cook over medium heat for 5–8 minutes, or until golden. Add the garlic, tomato, tomato paste, wine, sugar, lemon rind, half the basil and 1 cup (250 ml) water. Cook for 1 hour, stirring occasionally, or until the sauce is reduced and thickened. Season with salt and pepper.

Add the prawns and cook for 1 minute, then add the scallops and cook for 2 minutes. Stir in the calamari and cook for 1 minute more, or until all of the seafood is cooked through and tender.

Meanwhile, cook the spaghetti in lightly salted boiling water until *al dente*. Drain and toss with the sauce, parsley and remaining basil. Serve topped with shaved Parmesan.

Serves 4

Prawn, ricotta and spinach pasta

3 firm ripe tomatoes, peeled, seeded
  and finely chopped
½ cup (125 ml) extra virgin olive oil
½ cup (125 ml) balsamic vinegar
3 cloves garlic, finely chopped
3 tablespoons finely chopped fresh
  basil
500 g penne rigate
1 tablespoon olive oil
800 g raw medium prawns, peeled
  and deveined, with tails intact
100 g baby English spinach leaves
200 g firm ricotta, crumbled
2 tablespoons shaved Parmesan

Combine the tomato, extra virgin olive oil, 2 tablespoons of the balsamic vinegar, 1 clove of the garlic and 2 tablespoons of the basil.

Cook the pasta in a large saucepan of boiling water until *al dente*. Drain and keep warm.

Meanwhile, heat the olive oil in a frying pan over high heat, stir in the remaining garlic, then add the prawns and cook over high heat for 1–2 minutes, or until the prawns turn pink. Add the remaining vinegar and basil and cook for 1–2 minutes, or until the liquid has reduced and the prawns are cooked and slightly glazed. Stir in the spinach until just wilted. Season.

Toss together everything except the cheeses. Divide among bowls and top with the ricotta and Parmesan.

Serves 4

Penne with rustic lentil sauce

1 litre chicken stock
350 g penne
1/3 cup (80 ml) virgin olive oil, plus
  extra for drizzling
1 onion, chopped
2 carrots, diced
3 celery sticks, diced
3 cloves garlic, crushed
1 tablespoon plus 1 teaspoon
  chopped fresh thyme
400 g can lentils, drained

Boil the chicken stock in a large saucepan for 10 minutes, or until reduced to 2 cups (500 ml) of liquid. Meanwhile, cook the pasta in a large saucepan of rapidly boiling water until *al dente*. Drain and toss with 2 tablespoons of the olive oil.

Heat the remaining oil in a large, deep frying pan, add the onion, carrot and celery and cook over medium heat for 10 minutes, or until browned. Add two thirds of the crushed garlic and 1 tablespoon of the thyme and cook for a further minute. Add the stock, bring to the boil and cook for 8 minutes, or until reduced slightly and the vegetables are tender. Gently stir in the lentils until heated through.

Stir in the remaining garlic and thyme, and season with plenty of salt and black pepper—the stock should be slightly syrupy at this point. Combine the pasta with the lentil sauce in a large bowl, drizzle generously with virgin olive oil and serve with grated Parmesan, if desired.

Serves 4

Fettucine with creamy spinach and roast tomato

6 Roma (egg) tomatoes
40 g butter
2 cloves garlic, crushed
1 onion, chopped
500 g English spinach, trimmed
1 cup (250 ml) vegetable stock
1/2 cup (125 ml) thick cream
500 g fresh spinach fettucine
50 g shaved Parmesan

Preheat the oven to hot 220°C (425°F/Gas 7). Cut the tomatoes in half lengthways, then cut each half into three wedges. Place the wedges on a lightly greased baking tray and bake for 30–35 minutes, or until softened and slightly golden. Meanwhile, heat the butter in a large frying pan. Add the garlic and onion and cook over medium heat for 5 minutes, or until the onion is soft. Add the spinach, stock and cream, increase the heat to high and bring to the boil. Simmer rapidly for 5 minutes.

While the spinach mixture is cooking, cook the pasta in a large saucepan of boiling water until *al dente*. Drain and return to the pan. Remove the spinach from the heat and season well. Cool slightly, then process in a food processor until smooth. Toss through the pasta until well coated. Divide among serving bowls, top with the roasted tomatoes and Parmesan.

Serves 4–6

Roasted tomato and ricotta tagliatelle

12 Roma (egg) tomatoes, halved
  lengthways
½ cup (125 ml) olive oil
¼ teaspoon sugar
500 g fresh tagliatelle
2 cloves garlic, thinly sliced
300 g fresh ricotta
½ cup (15 g) fresh basil, shredded
½ cup (50 g) grated Parmesan
2 teaspoons olive oil, extra

Preheat the oven to moderately hot 200°C (400°F/Gas 6). Place the tomatoes cut-side-up in a single layer in a large roasting tin and brush with 2 tablespoons oil. Sprinkle with the sugar, and season. Bake for 1 hour, or until soft.

Meanwhile, cook the pasta in a large saucepan of lightly salted boiling water until *al dente*.

Heat the remaining oil in a frying pan, add the garlic and cook for 1–2 minutes, or until lightly golden. Drain the pasta, leaving it slightly wet, and place it in a large bowl with the tomato, garlic and oil from the pan, ricotta, basil and Parmesan, and mix together well. Season with salt and freshly ground black pepper. Drizzle with the extra olive oil and serve.

Serves 4

Variation: Stir in 50 g toasted pine nuts before serving.

Linguine with ham, artichoke and lemon sauce

500 g fresh linguine
25 g butter
2 large cloves garlic, chopped
150 g marinated artichokes, drained
  and quartered
150 g sliced leg ham, cut into strips
300 ml cream
2 teaspoons coarsely grated lemon
  rind
1/2 cup (15 g) fresh basil, torn
1/3 cup (35 g) grated Parmesan

Cook the pasta in a large saucepan of boiling water until *al dente*. Drain, then return to the pan. Meanwhile, melt the butter in a large frying pan, add the garlic and cook over medium heat for 1 minute, or until fragrant. Add the artichokes and ham and cook for a further 2 minutes.

Add the cream and lemon zest, reduce the heat and simmer for 5 minutes, gently breaking up the artichokes with a wooden spoon. Pour the sauce over the pasta, then add the basil and Parmesan and toss well until the pasta is evenly coated. Divide among four serving plates and serve immediately.

Serves 4

Won ton chicken ravioli with a Thai dressing

400 g chicken mince
2 spring onions, finely chopped
3 kaffir lime leaves, very finely
　shredded
2 tablespoons sweet chilli sauce
3 tablespoons chopped fresh
　coriander leaves
1½ teaspoons sesame oil
2 teaspoons grated lime rind
270 g packet won ton wrappers
½ cup (125 ml) fish sauce
2 tablespoons grated palm sugar
　or soft brown sugar
1 tablespoon peanut oil
1 tablespoon lime juice
finely chopped fresh red chilli,
　to garnish
chopped fresh coriander leaves,
　to garnish

Combine the mince, spring onion, lime leaves, chilli sauce, coriander, sesame oil and lime rind in a bowl.

Place a tablespoon of the mixture in the centre of a won ton wrapper, brush the edges lightly with water and top with another wrapper, pressing down around the edges to stop the ravioli from opening during cooking. Repeat with the remaining filling and wrappers.

Cook the ravioli in batches in a large saucepan of boiling water for 5 minutes, or until *al dente* and the chicken mince is cooked, then drain well and place on serving plates.

Combine the fish sauce, palm sugar, peanut oil and lime juice in a bowl. Pour over the ravioli and garnish with the chilli and coriander.

Serves 4 as an entrée

Bucatini with sausage and fennel seed

500 g good-quality Italian sausages
2 tablespoons olive oil
3 cloves garlic, chopped
1 teaspoon fennel seeds
½ teaspoon chilli flakes
2 x 425 g cans crushed tomatoes
500 g bucatini pasta
1 teaspoon balsamic vinegar
¼ cup (7 g) loosely packed fresh
   basil, chopped

Heat a frying pan over high heat, add the sausages and cook, turning, for 8–10 minutes, or until well browned and cooked through. Remove, cool slightly and slice on the diagonal into 1 cm pieces.

Heat the oil in a saucepan, add the garlic and cook over medium heat for 1 minute. Add the fennel seeds and chilli flakes and cook for a further minute. Stir in the tomato and bring to the boil, then reduce the heat and simmer, covered, for 20 minutes. Meanwhile, cook the pasta in a large saucepan of boiling water until *al dente*. Drain and return to the pan to keep warm.

Add the sausages to the sauce and cook, uncovered, for 5 minutes to heat through. Stir in the balsamic vinegar and basil. Divide the pasta among four bowls, top with the sauce and serve.

Serves 4

Prawn, tomato and saffron pasta

400 g tagliatelle
2 tablespoons olive oil
1 onion, diced
3 cloves garlic, chopped with
  1 teaspoon salt
2 pinches of saffron threads
1 red capsicum, diced
1 kg raw medium prawns, peeled
  and deveined, with tails intact
300 ml cream
1/4 cup (60 ml) dry white wine
1/4 cup (60 ml) fish or chicken stock
5 Roma tomatoes, peeled, seeded
  and diced
1 cup (60 g) roughly chopped fresh
  basil
2 tablespoons chopped fresh
  flat-leaf parsley
40 g Parmesan shavings

Cook the pasta in a large saucepan of boiling salted water until *al dente*. Drain and keep warm.

Meanwhile, heat the oil in a frying pan, add the onion, garlic, saffron and capsicum and stir over medium heat for 2 minutes before adding the prawns. Cook for 2–3 minutes, or until pink and cooked. Remove the prawns with tongs and set aside.

Add the cream, wine, stock and tomato to the pan and cook for 10 minutes, or until reduced slightly. Add the herbs and the cooked prawns. Season.

Toss with the pasta and serve topped with Parmesan shavings.

Serves 4–6

Spaghettini with herbs, baby spinach and garlic crumbs

375 g spaghettini
125 g day-old crusty Italian bread, crusts removed
100 ml extra virgin olive oil, plus extra for drizzling
4 cloves garlic, finely chopped
400 g baby spinach leaves
1/2 cup (25 g) chopped fresh flat-leaf parsley
4 tablespoons chopped fresh basil
1 tablespoon fresh thyme leaves
30 g shaved Parmesan

Cook the pasta in a large saucepan of boiling water until *al dente*. Drain, reserving 1/2 cup (125 ml) of the pasta water. Return the pasta to the saucepan and keep warm.

To make the garlic breadcrumbs, place the crustless bread in a food processor or blender and pulse until coarse breadcrumbs form. Heat 1 tablespoon of the oil in a saucepan. Add the breadcrumbs and half the garlic and toss for 2–3 minutes, or until lightly golden. Remove, then wipe the pan clean with paper towel.

Heat 2 tablespoons of the oil in the same pan. Add the spinach and remaining garlic, toss together for 1 minute, then add the herbs. Cook, tossing frequently, for a further 1 minute to wilt the herbs a little and to heat through. Toss the spinach mixture through the pasta with the remaining oil and reserved pasta water. Divide among four serving bowls and scatter with the garlic crumbs. Serve hot sprinkled with Parmesan and drizzled with extra virgin olive oil.

Serves 4

Creamy pesto chicken penne

1 tablespoon oil
40 g butter
400 g chicken breast fillets
170 g thin asparagus, cut into
  4 cm lengths
3 spring onions, chopped
4 cloves garlic, crushed
½ cup (125 ml) cream
300 g sour cream
¾ cup (185 ml) chicken stock
1 cup (100 g) grated Parmesan
½ cup (30 g) finely chopped fresh
  basil
2 tablespoons toasted pine nuts
400 g penne pasta
fresh basil leaves, to garnish

Heat the oil and half the butter in a large frying pan over high heat. Add the chicken and cook for 5 minutes on each side, or until just cooked. Remove, cover and cool, then cut into 1 cm slices.

Add the asparagus and spring onion to the pan, and cook for 2 minutes, or until the asparagus is just tender. Remove. Wipe out the pan with paper towels.

Reduce the heat to medium, add the remaining butter and the garlic, and cook for 2 minutes, or until pale gold. Add the cream, sour cream and stock, and simmer for 10 minutes, or until reduced slightly. Add the Parmesan and basil, and stir for 2 minutes, or until the cheese has melted. Return the chicken and asparagus to the pan, add the pine nuts and cook for 2 minutes to heat through. Season.

Meanwhile, cook the pasta in a large saucepan of lightly salted boiling water until *al dente*. Drain well. Combine the sauce and the pasta and garnish with basil leaves.

Serves 4

Pasta with baby spinach, pumpkin and tomato

750 g sweet pumpkin (e.g. butternut
  or jap)
2 tablespoons Parmesan-infused
  olive oil (see Notes)
16 unpeeled cloves garlic
250 g cherry tomatoes, halved
500 g orecchiette or penne pasta
200 g baby English spinach leaves
200 g marinated Persian feta
  (see Notes)
¼ cup (60 ml) sherry vinegar
2 tablespoons walnut oil

Preheat the oven to moderately
hot 200°C (400°F/Gas 6). Cut the
pumpkin into large cubes, place
in a roasting tin and drizzle with
Parmesan oil. Roast for 30 minutes,
then add the garlic. Arrange the
tomatoes on a baking tray. Place
the vegetables in the oven and roast
for 10–15 minutes, or until cooked.
Don't overcook the tomatoes or they
will turn to mush.

Meanwhile, cook the pasta in a
large saucepan of boiling water
until *al dente*. Drain well.

Toss together the pasta, tomatoes,
pumpkin, garlic and spinach in a
large bowl. Drain the feta, reserving
¼ cup (60 ml) marinade. Whisk the
reserved marinade, sherry vinegar
and walnut oil together. Pour over
the pasta and sprinkle with pieces
of the cheese.

Serves 4

Notes: Parmesan-infused olive oil
is available at gourmet food stores
and really adds depth of flavour.
Persian feta is softer and creamier
than other feta and is marinated
in oil, herbs and garlic.
Variation: Toss in 200 g marinated
Kalamata olives for added flavour.

Veal tortellini with creamy mushroom sauce

500 g veal tortellini
¼ cup (60 ml) olive oil
600 g Swiss brown mushrooms,
   thinly sliced
2 cloves garlic, crushed
½ cup (125 ml) dry white wine
300 ml thick cream
pinch ground nutmeg
3 tablespoons finely chopped
   fresh flat-leaf parsley
30 g grated Parmesan

Cook the pasta in a large saucepan of boiling water until *al dente*. Drain. Meanwhile, heat the oil in a frying pan over medium heat. Add the mushrooms and cook, stirring occasionally, for 5 minutes, or until softened. Add the garlic and cook for 1 minute, then stir in the wine and cook for 5 minutes, or until the liquid has reduced by half.

Combine the cream, nutmeg and parsley, add to the sauce and cook for 3–5 minutes, or until the sauce thickens slightly. Season. Divide the tortellini among four serving plates and spoon on the mushroom sauce. Sprinkle with Parmesan and serve.

Serves 4

Sweet potato gnocchi with wilted greens

500 g russet or sebago potatoes,
  chopped
250 g orange sweet potato, chopped
1 egg yolk
2 tablespoons milk
1/4 teaspoon ground nutmeg
1 1/4 cups (155 g) plain flour
1 tablespoon olive oil
4 rashers bacon, thinly sliced
1 small onion, chopped
1/3 cup (80 ml) sweet sherry
500 g English spinach
40 g butter
2 tablespoons toasted pine nuts

Preheat the oven to hot 220°C (425°F/Gas 7). Bake the potato and sweet potato in a roasting tin for 40–60 minutes, or until soft. Cut in half and leave for 10 minutes. While still warm, press through a sieve into a large bowl. Add the egg yolk and milk, then the nutmeg, 1 cup (125 g) flour and 1 1/4 teaspoons salt, and mix well to combine.

Lightly knead the mixture until it is smooth, adding more flour if it gets sticky. Roll into 2 cm cylinders, then cut into 2 cm diagonal lengths. Indent on one side with a fork.

Heat the oil in a large frying pan, add the bacon and onion, and cook over medium heat for 5 minutes, or until the onion is just golden. Add the sherry, stir well and cook for 2 minutes, or until reduced slightly. Add the spinach and cook, stirring, for 2 minutes, or until wilted, but still bright green. Stir in the butter and season. Keep warm.

Cook the gnocchi in boiling water in batches for 2–3 minutes, or until they rise to the surface. Drain and toss through the sauce. Scatter the pine nuts over the top.

Serves 4

Spaghetti Bolognese

60 g butter
1 onion, finely chopped
2 cloves garlic, crushed
1 celery stick, finely chopped
1 carrot, diced
50 g piece pancetta, diced
500 g minced beef
1 tablespoon chopped fresh oregano
1 cup (250 ml) red wine
2 cups (500 ml) beef stock
2 tablespoons tomato paste
2 x 400 g cans crushed tomatoes
400 g spaghetti
3 tablespoons grated reggiano
  Parmesan

Melt the butter in a large saucepan, add the onion and cook over medium heat for 2–3 minutes, or until it starts to soften. Add the garlic, celery and carrot, and cook, stirring, over low heat, for 5 minutes. Increase the heat to high, add the pancetta, beef and oregano, and cook for 4–5 minutes, or until browned. Use a fork to break up any lumps.

Pour in the wine, reduce the heat and simmer for 4–5 minutes, or until it is absorbed. Add the stock, tomato paste and tomato, and season well. Cover with a lid and simmer for 1½ hours, stirring occasionally to prevent the sauce from catching on the bottom of the saucepan. Uncover and simmer for another hour, stirring occasionally.

Cook the spaghetti in a large saucepan of boiling water until *al dente*. Drain, divide among four serving plates and top with the sauce. Sprinkle with the Parmesan and serve.

Serves 4

Cresti di gallo with creamy tomato and bacon sauce

400 g cresti di gallo pasta
1 tablespoon olive oil
170 g streaky bacon, thinly sliced (see Note)
500 g Roma tomatoes, roughly chopped
1/2 cup (125 ml) thick cream
2 tablespoons sun-dried tomato pesto
2 tablespoons finely chopped fresh flat-leaf parsley
1/2 cup (50 g) finely grated Parmesan

Cook the pasta in a large saucepan of boiling water until *al dente*. Drain well and return to the saucepan. Meanwhile, heat the oil in a frying pan, add the bacon and cook over high heat for 2 minutes, or until starting to brown. Reduce the heat to medium, add the tomato and cook, stirring frequently, for 2 minutes, or until the tomato has softened but still holds its shape.

Add the cream and tomato pesto and stir until heated through. Remove from the heat, add the parsley, then toss the sauce through the pasta with the grated Parmesan.

Serves 4

Note: Streaky bacon is the tail ends of bacon rashers. It is fattier but adds to the flavour of the meal. You can use 170 g bacon rashers if preferred.

Roast pumpkin sauce on pappardelle

1.4 kg butternut pumpkin, cut
   into 2 cm pieces
4 cloves garlic, crushed
3 teaspoons fresh thyme leaves
100 ml olive oil
500 g pappardelle pasta
2 tablespoons cream
3/4 cup (185 ml) hot chicken stock
30 g shaved Parmesan

Preheat the oven to moderately hot 200°C (400°F/Gas 6). Place the pumpkin, garlic, thyme and 1/4 cup (60 ml) of the olive oil in a bowl and toss together. Season with salt, transfer to a baking tray and cook for 30 minutes, or until tender and golden. Meanwhile, cook the pasta in a large saucepan of boiling water until *al dente*. Drain and return to the pan. Toss through the remaining oil and keep warm.

Place the cooked pumpkin and the cream in a food processor or blender and process until smooth. Add the hot stock and process until smooth and combined. Season with salt and cracked black pepper and gently toss through the warm pasta. Divide among four serving plates, sprinkle with Parmesan and extra thyme, if desired, and serve immediately.

Serves 4

Note: The sauce becomes gluggy on standing, so serve it as soon as possible.

Tagliatelle with chicken, herbs and mushrooms

2 tablespoons olive oil
350 g chicken tenderloins, cut
   into 2 cm pieces
20 g butter
400 g mushrooms, sliced
2 cloves garlic, finely chopped
½ cup (125 ml) dry white wine
¾ cup (185 ml) cream
400 g tagliatelle
1 teaspoon finely grated lemon rind
2 tablespoons lemon juice
2 tablespoons chopped fresh
   marjoram
2 tablespoons chopped fresh parsley
100 g grated Parmesan

Heat 1 tablespoon oil in a large frying pan, add the chicken and cook over medium heat for 3–4 minutes, or until lightly browned. Remove.

Heat the butter and remaining oil, add the mushrooms and cook, stirring, over high heat for 3 minutes. Add the garlic and cook for another 2 minutes.

Stir in the wine, reduce the heat and simmer for 5 minutes, or until nearly evaporated. Stir in the cream and chicken, and simmer for 5 minutes, or until thickened.

Meanwhile, cook the tagliatelle in lightly salted boiling water until *al dente*. Drain. Keep warm.

Stir the lemon rind and juice, marjoram, parsley and 2 tablespoons Parmesan into the sauce. Season, combine with the pasta and serve with the remaining Parmesan.

Serves 4

Spaghetti with smoked tuna and olives

800 g vine-ripened tomatoes
375 g spaghetti
3 x 125 g cans smoked tuna slices
  in oil
1 red onion, chopped
2 cloves garlic, crushed
1 teaspoon sugar
1 cup black olives
2 tablespoons chopped fresh basil
75 g Greek feta, crumbled

Score a cross in the base of each tomato. Place the tomatoes in a bowl of boiling water for 1 minute, then plunge into cold water and peel the skin away from the cross. Cut in half and remove the seeds with a teaspoon. Roughly chop the flesh. Cook the pasta in a large saucepan of boiling water until *al dente*. Drain and keep warm.

Drain the oil from the tuna slices, reserving 1 tablespoon. Heat the reserved oil in a large saucepan, add the onion and cook over low heat for 3–4 minutes, or until soft but not brown. Add the garlic and cook for another minute, then add the chopped tomatoes and sugar. Cook over medium heat for 8–10 minutes, or until pulpy.

Add the tuna slices, olives and chopped basil, stir well and cook for 2 minutes, or until warmed through. Toss through the spaghetti and season with salt and cracked black pepper. Sprinkle with crumbled feta and serve immediately.

Serves 4

Rice

Risi e bisi

1.25 litres chicken stock
bouquet garni (1 sprig fresh thyme,
    1 bay leaf, 2 stalks fresh flat-leaf
    parsley)
2 tablespoons olive oil
1 onion, chopped
1/2 celery stick, chopped
60 g pancetta, chopped
250 g arborio rice
300 g frozen baby peas
60 g unsalted butter
80 g grated Parmesan
shaved Parmesan, to serve

Place the stock and bouquet garni in a large saucepan with 3 cups (750 ml) water. Bring to the boil, then reduce the heat and simmer.

Heat the oil in a large frying pan, add the onion, celery and pancetta, and cook for 3–5 minutes, or until the onion is soft. Add the rice and stir for 1 minute, or until coated.

Remove the bouquet garni and add 1/2 cup (125 ml) hot stock to the rice, stirring constantly until all the stock is absorbed. Add another 1/2 cup (125 ml) stock and stir until all the stock is absorbed. Add the peas. Continue adding stock, 1/2 cup (125 ml) at a time, stirring, for 20–25 minutes, or until the rice is tender. The texture should be a little wetter than risotto, but not too soupy. Remove from the heat and stir in the butter and grated Parmesan. Season. Garnish with shaved Parmesan.

Serves 4

Chicken and mushroom risotto

1.25 litres vegetable or chicken stock
2 tablespoons olive oil
300 g chicken breast fillets, cut into
  1.5 cm wide strips
250 g small button mushrooms,
  halved
pinch nutmeg
2 cloves garlic, crushed
20 g butter
1 small onion, finely chopped
375 g arborio rice
2/3 cup (170 ml) dry white wine
3 tablespoons sour cream
3 tablespoons finely chopped fresh
  flat-leaf parsley
45 g freshly grated Parmesan

Bring the stock to the boil, reduce the heat and keep at a simmer. Heat the oil in a large saucepan. Cook the chicken over high heat for 3–4 minutes or until golden brown. Add the mushrooms and cook for 1–2 minutes more, or until starting to brown. Stir in the nutmeg and garlic, and season with salt and pepper. Cook for 30 seconds then remove from the pan and set aside.

Melt the butter in the same pan and cook the onion over low heat for 5–6 minutes. Add the rice, stir to coat, then add the wine. Once the wine is absorbed, reduce the heat and add 1/2 cup (125 ml) of the stock. When it is absorbed, add another 1/2 cup (125 ml). Continue adding stock for 20–25 minutes, or until all the stock has been used and the rice is creamy. Add the mushrooms and the chicken with the last of the stock.

Remove the pan from the heat, and stir in the sour cream, parsley and Parmesan. Check the seasoning then cover and leave for 2 minutes before serving.

Serves 4

Asparagus and pistachio risotto

1 litre vegetable stock
1 cup (250 ml) white wine
⅓ cup (80 ml) extra virgin olive oil
1 red onion, finely chopped
2 cups (440 g) arborio rice
310 g asparagus spears, trimmed
  and cut into 3 cm pieces
½ cup (125 ml) cream
1 cup (100 g) grated Parmesan
½ cup (40 g) shelled pistachio nuts,
  toasted and roughly chopped

Heat the stock and wine in a large saucepan, bring to the boil, then reduce the heat, cover and keep at a low simmer.

Heat the oil in another saucepan. Add the onion and cook over medium heat for 3 minutes, or until soft. Add the rice and stir for 1 minute, or until the rice is translucent.

Add ½ cup (125 ml) hot stock, stirring constantly over medium heat until the liquid is absorbed. Continue adding stock, ½ cup (125 ml) at a time, stirring constantly for 20–25 minutes, or until all the stock is absorbed and the rice is tender and creamy. Add the asparagus pieces during the final 5 minutes of cooking. Remove from the heat.

Stand for 2 minutes, stir in the cream and Parmesan and season to taste with salt and black pepper. Serve sprinkled with pistachios.

Serves 4–6

Chicken gumbo

30 g butter
2 rashers bacon, thinly sliced
1 small onion, chopped
1 small green capsicum, diced
2 cloves garlic, chopped
1/4 teaspoon cayenne pepper
600 g chicken breast fillets, cubed
1/4 teaspoon saffron threads, soaked
   in 2 tablespoons warm water
1 tablespoon brandy
1 tablespoon tomato paste
2 tablespoons plain flour
1 litre chicken stock
3/4 cup (150 g) basmati rice
1 tablespoon olive oil
400 g raw small prawns, peeled,
   deveined, tails intact
300 g okra, thickly sliced
2 tablespoons cream
3 tablespoons chopped fresh
   flat-leaf parsley
1/2 teaspoon Tabasco sauce

Melt the butter in a large saucepan over medium heat, add the bacon, onion, capsicum, garlic, cayenne and chicken, and cook, stirring, for 5–8 minutes, or until light golden. Stir in the saffron and soaking liquid, the brandy, tomato paste and flour, and cook, stirring constantly, for 3 minutes.

Gradually add the stock and bring to the boil. Add the rice, then reduce the heat to low and simmer gently for 10 minutes.

Meanwhile, heat the olive oil in a separate saucepan, add the prawns and okra, and toss quickly together for 1–2 minutes, or until the prawns change colour. Add to the gumbo, then stir in the cream, parsley and Tabasco, and heat for 1–2 minutes. Serve in deep bowls with corn bread.

Serves 4–6

Chicken and mushroom pilau

1½ cups (300 g) basmati rice
2 tablespoons oil
1 large onion, chopped
3–4 cloves garlic, crushed
1 tablespoon finely chopped
  fresh ginger
500 g chicken tenderloin fillets,
  trimmed and cut into small pieces
300 g Swiss brown mushrooms,
  sliced
¾ cup (90 g) slivered almonds,
  toasted
1½–2 teaspoons garam masala,
  dry roasted
½ cup (125 g) plain yoghurt
1 tablespoon finely chopped fresh
  coriander leaves
fresh coriander leaves, extra,
  to garnish

Rinse the rice under cold water until the water runs clear. Drain and leave for 30 minutes. Heat the oil in a large saucepan and stir in the onion, garlic and ginger. Reduce the heat to medium and cook, covered, for 5 minutes, or until the onion has browned. Increase the heat to high, add the chicken and cook, stirring, for 3–4 minutes, or until the chicken is lightly browned. Stir in the sliced mushrooms, almonds and garam masala. Cook, covered, for another 3 minutes, or until the mushrooms are soft. Uncover and cook without stirring for 2 minutes, or until the liquid has evaporated.

Remove the chicken from the pan. Add the rice and stir for 30 seconds, or until well coated in the mushroom and onion mixture. Pour in 1½ cups (375 ml) water and bring to the boil, stirring frequently, for 2 minutes, or until most of the water evaporates. Return the chicken to the pan. Cover, reduce the heat to low and steam for 15 minutes, or until the rice is cooked.

Combine the yoghurt and chopped coriander. Fluff the rice with a fork, and divide among serving bowls. Top with a dollop of the yoghurt mixture and garnish with coriander leaves.

Serves 4–6

Paella

500 g black mussels
1/4 cup (60 ml) olive oil
600 g chicken drumettes or thigh
  fillets, halved
1 onion, chopped
2 large cloves garlic, chopped
3 vine-ripened tomatoes, peeled,
  seeded and finely chopped
1 small red capsicum, diced
1 small green capsicum, diced
1/4 teaspoon chilli flakes
1 teaspoon paprika
1/4 teaspoon saffron threads soaked
  in 1/4 cup (60 ml) warm water
1 1/3 cups (290 g) short-grain rice
1 litre vegetable stock
12 raw medium prawns, peeled,
  deveined, tails intact
1 cup (155 g) peas
1/4 cup (60 ml) dry sherry
1/2 cup (30 g) chopped fresh parsley
1 lemon, cut into wedges

Scrub the mussels and remove the beards. Discard any open mussels that don't close when tapped.

Heat 2 tablespoons oil in a large frying pan, add the chicken and cook over medium heat for 5–7 minutes, or until browned. Remove. Add the remaining oil to the pan, then add the onion, garlic and tomato, and cook over low heat for 5 minutes, or until soft. Do not brown. Add the capsicum and cook for 1 minute, then stir in the chilli flakes, paprika and saffron and its soaking liquid. Pour in the rice and return the chicken to the pan. Add the stock, bring to the boil, then reduce the heat and simmer for 10 minutes.

Stir in the prawns, peas, sherry and mussels. Cover for 2 minutes, or until the mussels open. Discard any that do not open. Stir for 2 minutes, or until the prawns are pink and cooked through. Stir in the parsley. Serve immediately with the lemon wedges.

Serves 4

Risotto with scallops and minted peas

1 litre chicken, fish or vegetable stock
2¾ cups (360 g) fresh or frozen
  baby peas
2 tablespoons light sour cream
2 tablespoons finely shredded fresh
  mint
1 tablespoon olive oil
1 small onion, finely chopped
2 cloves garlic, finely chopped
150 g arborio rice
16 large scallops (without roe)
1 tablespoon grated fresh Parmesan
4 fresh mint leaves, to garnish
lemon wedges, to serve

Bring the stock to the boil, and add the peas. Simmer for 1–2 minutes, or until the peas are tender, then remove, keeping the stock at a low simmer. Blend 1¾ cups (230 g) of the peas with the sour cream in a food processor until smooth. Season, then stir in 1 tablespoon of the mint.

Place the oil in a shallow saucepan and cook the onion over low heat for 4–5 minutes, or until soft. Add the garlic and cook for 30 seconds. Stir in the rice to coat. Increase the heat to medium.

Add 1 cup (250 ml) stock to the rice mixture and cook, stirring constantly, until the liquid has evaporated. Add the stock, ½ cup (125 ml) at a time until the rice is tender and creamy. This will take about 20 minutes. Meanwhile, season the scallops and heat a chargrill pan or hotplate. Add the scallops and sear on both sides until cooked to your liking.

Fold the pea purée through the risotto with the reserved whole peas and Parmesan. Divide the risotto among the serving bowls and top with the scallops. Sprinkle with the remaining mint, garnish with a mint leaf and serve with a wedge of lemon.

Serves 4–6

Green pilau with cashews

200 g baby English spinach leaves
$^2/_3$ cup (100 g) cashew nuts, chopped
2 tablespoons olive oil
6 spring onions, chopped
1$^1/_2$ cups (300 g) long-grain brown rice
2 cloves garlic, finely chopped
1 teaspoon fennel seeds
2 tablespoons lemon juice
2$^1/_2$ cups (625 ml) vegetable stock
3 tablespoons chopped fresh mint
3 tablespoons chopped fresh flat-leaf parsley

Preheat the oven to moderate 180°C (350°F/Gas 4). Shred the spinach into 1 cm slices.

Place the cashew nuts on a baking tray and roast for 5–10 minutes, or until golden brown — watch carefully or they will burn.

Heat the oil in a large frying pan and cook the spring onion over medium heat for 2 minutes, or until soft. Add the rice, garlic and fennel seeds and cook, stirring frequently, for 1–2 minutes, or until the rice is evenly coated. Increase the heat to high, add the lemon juice, stock and 1 teaspoon salt and bring to the boil. Reduce to low, cover and cook for 45 minutes without lifting the lid.

Remove from the heat and sprinkle with the spinach and herbs. Stand, covered, for 8 minutes, then fork the spinach and herbs through the rice. Season. Serve sprinkled with cashews.

Serves 6

Lemon and zucchini risotto

1.25 litres hot vegetable or chicken
  stock
2 tablespoons olive oil
1 onion, finely chopped
1²/₃ cups (360 g) arborio rice
¹/₃ cup (80 ml) dry sherry
3 teaspoons grated lemon rind
2 tablespoons lemon juice
350 g zucchini, diced
2 tablespoons chopped fresh
  flat-leaf parsley
¹/₂ cup (50 g) freshly grated Parmesan
lemon zest, to garnish

Place the stock in a large saucepan, bring to the boil, then reduce the heat, cover, and keep at a low simmer.

Heat the oil in a large saucepan, add the onion and cook over medium heat for 5 minutes, or until softened. Reduce the heat, stir in the rice and cook for 1 minute, stirring constantly.

Add ¹/₂ cup (125 ml) hot stock, stirring until all the stock is absorbed. Continue adding the stock, ¹/₂ cup (125 ml) at a time, stirring constantly, for 20 minutes, or until all the liquid is absorbed. If the risotto gets too dry add a little extra stock or water. Stir in the sherry, lemon rind, lemon juice and zucchini. Cook over low heat for a further 5 minutes, or until the risotto is tender, with a slight bite to the inside of the grain. Season with salt and freshly ground black pepper, and stir in the parsley and half the Parmesan. Garnish with the lemon zest and remaining Parmesan.

Serves 4

Chicken and pork paella

¼ cup (60 ml) olive oil
1 large red capsicum, seeded and
  cut into 5 mm strips
600 g chicken thigh fillets, cut into
  3 cm cubes
200 g chorizo sausage, cut into
  2 cm slices
200 g mushrooms, thinly sliced
3 cloves garlic, crushed
1 tablespoon lemon zest
700 g tomatoes, roughly chopped
200 g green beans, cut into 3 cm
  lengths
1 tablespoon chopped fresh
  rosemary
2 tablespoons chopped fresh flat-leaf
  parsley
¼ teaspoon saffron threads dissolved
  in ¼ cup (60 ml) hot water
2 cups (440 g) short-grain rice
3 cups (750 ml) hot chicken stock
6 lemon wedges

Heat the olive oil in a large, deep
frying pan or paella pan over medium
heat. Add the capsicum and cook for
6 minutes, or until softened. Remove
from the pan. Add the chicken to
the pan and cook for 10 minutes,
or until brown on all sides. Remove.
Add the sausage to the pan and cook
for 5 minutes, or until golden on all
sides. Remove.

Add the mushrooms, garlic and lemon
zest, and cook over medium heat for
5 minutes. Stir in the tomato and
capsicum, and cook for a further
5 minutes, or until the tomato is soft.

Add the beans, rosemary, parsley,
saffron mixture, rice, chicken and
sausage. Stir briefly and add the
stock. Do not stir. Reduce the heat
and simmer for 30 minutes. Remove
from the heat, cover and leave to
stand for 10 minutes. Serve with
lemon wedges.

Serves 6

Note: Paellas are not stirred right to
the bottom of the pan during cooking
in the hope that a thin crust of crispy
rice will form. This is considered one
of the best parts of the paella. For
this reason, it is important to not
use a non-stick frying pan.

Asian barley pilau

15 g dried sliced mushrooms
2 cups (500 ml) vegetable stock
1/2 cup (125 ml) dry sherry
1 tablespoon oil
3 large French shallots, thinly sliced
2 large cloves garlic, crushed
1 tablespoon grated fresh ginger
1 teaspoon Sichuan peppercorns,
  crushed
1 1/2 cups (330 g) pearl barley
500 g choy sum, cut into 5 cm
  lengths
3 teaspoons kecap manis
1 teaspoon sesame oil

Place the mushrooms in a bowl and cover with boiling water, then leave for 15 minutes. Strain, reserving 1/2 cup (125 ml) of the liquid.

Bring the stock and sherry to the boil in a saucepan, then reduce the heat, cover and simmer until needed.

Heat the oil in a large saucepan and cook the shallots over medium heat for 2–3 minutes, or until soft. Add the garlic, ginger and peppercorns and cook for 1 minute. Add the barley and mushrooms and mix well. Stir in the stock and mushroom liquid, then reduce the heat and simmer, covered, for 25 minutes, or until all of the liquid evaporates.

Meanwhile, steam the choy sum until wilted. Add to the barley mixture. Stir in the kecap manis and sesame oil.

Serves 4

Pumpkin risotto

600 g pumpkin, cut into 1 cm cubes
3 tablespoons olive oil
2 cups (500 ml) vegetable stock
1 onion, finely chopped
2 cloves garlic, finely chopped
1 tablespoon chopped fresh
  rosemary
2 cups (440 g) arborio rice
½ cup (125 ml) white wine
30 g butter
⅓ cup (35 g) grated Parmesan
3 tablespoons finely chopped fresh
  flat-leaf parsley

Preheat the oven to moderately hot 200°C (400°F/Gas 6). Toss the pieces of pumpkin in 2 tablespoons of the oil, place in a baking dish and roast for 30 minutes, or until tender and golden. Turn the pumpkin pieces halfway through the cooking time.

Heat the stock and 3 cups (750 ml) water in a saucepan, cover and keep at a low simmer.

Heat the remaining oil in a large saucepan and cook the onion, garlic and rosemary, stirring, over low heat for 5 minutes, or until the onion is cooked but not browned. Add the rice and stir to coat. Stir in the wine for 2–3 minutes, or until absorbed.

Add ½ cup (125 ml) stock, stirring constantly over medium heat until all the liquid is absorbed. Continue adding the stock ½ cup (125 ml) at a time, stirring constantly, for 20 minutes, or until all the stock is absorbed and the rice is tender and creamy. Season to taste with salt and black pepper, and stir in the pumpkin, butter, Parmesan and parsley. Serve immediately.

Serves 4–6

Prawn pilau

2 cups (400 g) basmati rice
60 g butter
1 onion, finely chopped
2 cloves garlic, finely chopped
1 cm x 4 cm piece fresh ginger,
   peeled and grated
1 fresh green chilli, finely chopped
3 teaspoons coriander seeds
1 teaspoon ground turmeric
2 cardamom pods, cracked
1 kg raw medium prawns, peeled
   and deveined, with tails intact
1/2 cup (80 g) raw cashew nuts
1/3 cup (80 ml) lemon juice
1/2 cup (25 g) chopped fresh
   coriander leaves

Rinse the rice under cold water until the water runs clear. Drain well. Melt 30 g butter over low heat in a large saucepan; add the onion and cook for 3 minutes, or until soft. Add the garlic, ginger, chilli, coriander seeds and turmeric, and cook for 2 minutes.

Add the rice to the saucepan and cook for 1 minute, then add the cardamom pods and 1 litre water. Bring to the boil, then reduce the heat and simmer, covered, for 10 minutes, or until the rice is tender. Remove from the heat and leave, covered, for 5 minutes to steam.

Melt the remaining butter in a frying pan, and cook the prawns and cashew nuts over high heat for 3–4 minutes, or until the prawns are pink and cooked through. Add both to the pan with the rice, then add the lemon juice and coriander and stir everything together. Season to taste with salt and pepper, and serve.

Serves 4–6

Mushroom risotto

1.5 litres vegetable stock
2 cups (500 ml) white wine
2 tablespoons olive oil
60 g butter
2 leeks, thinly sliced
1 kg flat mushrooms, sliced
500 g arborio rice
3/4 cup (75 g) grated Parmesan
3 tablespoons chopped fresh
   flat-leaf parsley
balsamic vinegar, to serve
shaved Parmesan, to garnish
fresh flat-leaf parsley, to garnish

Place the stock and wine in a large saucepan, bring to the boil, then reduce the heat to low, cover and keep at a low simmer.

Meanwhile, heat the oil and butter in a large saucepan. Add the leek and cook over medium heat for 5 minutes, or until soft and golden. Add the mushrooms to the pan and cook for 5 minutes, or until tender. Add the rice and stir for 1 minute, or until the rice is translucent.

Add 1/2 cup (125 ml) of hot stock, stirring constantly, over medium heat until the liquid is absorbed. Continue adding more stock, 1/2 cup (125 ml) at a time, stirring constantly between additions, for 20–25 minutes, or until all the stock is absorbed and the rice is tender and creamy in texture.

Stir in the Parmesan and chopped parsley and heat for 1 minute, or until all the cheese is melted. Serve drizzled with balsamic vinegar and top with Parmesan shavings and garnish with the parsley.

Serves 4

Chicken and asparagus risotto

1.5 litres chicken stock
1 cup (250 ml) dry white wine
6 whole black peppercorns
2 bay leaves
1 tablespoon olive oil
40 g butter
600 g chicken breast fillets,
  cut into 2 cm cubes
1 leek, sliced
2 cloves garlic, crushed
2 cups (440 g) arborio rice
200 g asparagus, cut into 3 cm
  lengths
1/2 cup (50 g) grated Parmesan
2 tablespoons lemon juice
3 tablespoons chopped fresh parsley
shaved Parmesan, to garnish

Place the stock, wine, peppercorns and bay leaves in a saucepan, and simmer for 5 minutes. Strain, return to the pan and keep at a low simmer.

Heat the oil and half the butter in a saucepan, add the chicken and cook over medium heat for 5 minutes, or until golden. Remove. Add the leek and garlic and cook for 5 minutes, or until softened.

Add the rice and stir for 1 minute to coat. Add 1/2 cup (125 ml) stock, stirring until absorbed. Continue adding stock, 1/2 cup (125 ml) at a time, stirring constantly for 20–25 minutes, until the stock is absorbed and the rice is tender. Add the asparagus and chicken in the last 5 minutes.

When the chicken is cooked through, stir in the Parmesan, juice, parsley and remaining butter. Season, and garnish with the shaved Parmesan.

Serves 4

Rice and red lentil pilau

Garam masala
1 tablespoon coriander seeds
1 tablespoon cardamom pods
1 tablespoon cumin seeds
1 teaspoon whole black peppercorns
1 teaspoon whole cloves
1 small cinnamon stick, crushed

¼ cup (60 ml) oil
1 onion, chopped
3 cloves garlic, chopped
1 cup (200 g) basmati rice
1 cup (250 g) red lentils
3 cups (750 ml) hot vegetable stock
spring onions, thinly sliced on the
    diagonal, to garnish

To make the garam masala, place all of the spices in a dry frying pan and shake over medium heat for 1 minute, or until fragrant. Blend in a spice grinder or blender until a fine powder.

Heat the oil in a large saucepan. Add the onion, garlic and 3 teaspoons garam masala. Cook over medium heat for 3 minutes, or until the onion is soft.

Stir in the rice and lentils and cook for 2 minutes. Add the hot stock and stir well. Slowly bring to the boil, then reduce the heat and simmer, covered, for 15–20 minutes, or until the rice is cooked and all the stock has been absorbed. Gently fluff the rice with a fork. Garnish with spring onion.

Serves 4–6

Note: You can use ready-made garam masala instead of making it.

Chinese fried rice

¼ cup (60 ml) oil
2 eggs, lightly beaten
1 carrot, thinly sliced
1 red capsicum, diced
6 fresh baby corn, sliced
2 cloves garlic, crushed
100 g lap cheong sausages,
   sliced on the diagonal
½ cup (80 g) frozen peas
1.5 kg frozen cooked long-grain
   rice, thawed (see Note)
3 spring onions, thinly sliced
3½ tablespoons soy sauce
2 teaspoons sugar
2 teaspoons sesame oil

Heat a wok or large frying pan over high heat, add 1 tablespoon of the oil and swirl to coat. Add the egg and swirl to distribute evenly. Cook for 1–2 minutes, or until golden, then turn and cook the other side. Remove, leave until cool enough to handle, then roll up and thinly slice.

Heat the remaining oil over high heat, add the carrot and stir-fry for 1 minute, then add the capsicum and cook for another minute. Finally, add the corn, garlic, sausage and peas, and stir-fry for 1 minute.

Add the rice, spring onion and omelette, and mix, separating the rice grains. Stir over medium heat for 3–4 minutes, or until the rice is warmed through. Stir in the soy sauce, sugar and sesame oil, and toss. Serve hot.

Serves 4–6

Note: If you are not using frozen rice, you will need to cook 3 cups (600 g) rice, then cool.
Variation: Instead of lap cheong sausage, try Chinese barbecue pork, sliced ham or prawns.

Sweet potato and sage risotto

8 slices prosciutto
100 ml extra virgin olive oil
1 red onion, cut into thin wedges
600 g orange sweet potato, peeled,
    cut into 2.5 cm cubes
2 cups (440 g) arborio rice
1.25 litres hot chicken stock
3/4 cup (75 g) shredded Parmesan
3 tablespoons shredded fresh sage

Place the prosciutto slices on a tray and cook under a hot grill for 1–2 minutes each side, or until crispy.

Heat 1/4 cup (60 ml) oil in a large saucepan, add the onion and cook over medium heat for 2–3 minutes, or until softened. Add the sweet potato and rice, and stir through until well coated in the oil.

Add 1/2 cup (125 ml) hot chicken stock, stirring constantly over medium heat until the liquid is absorbed. Continue adding more stock, 1/2 cup (125 ml) at a time, stirring constantly for 20–25 minutes, or until all the stock is absorbed, and the rice is tender and creamy. Stir in the shredded Parmesan and 2 tablespoons of the sage. Season. Spoon into four bowls and drizzle with the remaining oil. Break the prosciutto into pieces and sprinkle over the top with the remaining sage. Top with shaved Parmesan, if desired. Serve immediately.

Serves 4

Jambalaya

1 tablespoon olive oil
2 chicken breast fillets,
  cut into 1.5 x 6 cm strips
1 red onion, sliced
3 rashers bacon, chopped
2 chorizo sausages, cut into
  1 cm diagonal slices
1 small red capsicum, sliced
1 small green capsicum, sliced
2 cloves garlic, finely chopped
1–2 teaspoons seeded, finely
  chopped fresh jalapeño chilli
1 teaspoon smoked paprika
3 teaspoons Cajun spice mix
2 cups (400 g) long-grain rice,
  washed
1 cup (250 ml) beer
4 vine-ripened tomatoes, peeled
  and quartered
3 cups (750 ml) chicken stock
1/2 teaspoon saffron threads, soaked
  in 1 tablespoon warm water
16 raw medium prawns, peeled,
  deveined, tails intact

Heat the oil in a large saucepan. Cook the chicken in batches over medium heat for 4 minutes, or until lightly browned. Remove.

Cook the onion for 3 minutes, then add the bacon and sausage, and cook for 4–5 minutes, or until browned. Add the capsicum and cook for 2 minutes, then add the garlic, chilli, paprika and Cajun spice mix, and cook for a further 2 minutes.

Add the rice and stir to coat. Add the beer and stir for 30 seconds to remove any sediment stuck to the pan. Stir in the tomato, stock, saffron and soaking liquid. Bring to the boil, reduce the heat and simmer, covered, for 10–12 minutes.

Add the prawns and chicken, stir to prevent sticking, and cook, covered, for 3–5 minutes, or until the rice is creamy and tender.

Serves 6

Baked prawn risotto with Thai flavours

300 ml stock (fish, chicken
   or vegetable)
1 stem lemon grass, bruised
4 fresh kaffir lime leaves, finely
   shredded
2 tablespoons oil
1 small red onion, thinly sliced
1½–2 tablespoons good-quality
   purchased Thai red curry paste
1½ cups (330 g) arborio rice
300 ml coconut cream
600 g raw prawns, peeled and
   deveined with tails intact

Preheat the oven to moderate 180°C (350°F/Gas 4). Pour the stock into a saucepan, add the lemon grass and half of the kaffir lime leaves. Bring to the boil then reduce the heat and simmer, covered, for 10 minutes.

Heat the oil in a flameproof casserole dish with a lid. Add the onion and cook over medium–low heat for 4–5 minutes, or until soft but not coloured. Stir in the curry paste and cook for a further minute, or until fragrant. Stir in the rice until well coated. Strain the stock into the rice then add the coconut cream. Cover and bake for 15 minutes.

Remove from the oven, stir the risotto well, then bake for a further 10–15 minutes. Add the prawns and mix them well into the rice—if the mixture looks a little dry add ½ cup (125 ml) stock or water. Bake for a further 10–15 minutes, or until the prawns are cooked through and the rice is tender. Serve the risotto in bowls garnished with the remaining shredded lime leaves.

Serves 4

Wok

Sweet chilli prawns

1 kg raw medium prawns
2 tablespoons peanut oil
1 cm x 3 cm piece fresh ginger,
  cut into julienne strips
2 cloves garlic, finely chopped
5 spring onions, cut into 3 cm lengths
1/3 cup (80 ml) chilli garlic sauce
2 tablespoons tomato sauce
2 tablespoons Chinese rice wine
  (see Notes)
1 tablespoon Chinese black vinegar
  or rice vinegar (see Notes)
1 tablespoon soy sauce
1 tablespoon soft brown sugar
1 teaspoon cornflour mixed with
  1/2 cup (125 ml) water
finely chopped spring onion,
  to garnish

Peel and devein the prawns, leaving the tails intact. Heat a wok until very hot, then add the oil and swirl to coat the side. Heat over high heat until smoking, then quickly add the ginger, garlic and spring onion and stir-fry for 1 minute. Add the prawns and cook for 2 minutes, or until they are just pink and starting to curl. Remove the prawns from the wok with tongs or a slotted spoon.

Put the chilli garlic sauce, tomato sauce, rice wine, vinegar, soy sauce, sugar and cornflour paste in a small jug and whisk together. Pour the sauce into the wok and cook, stirring, for 1–2 minutes, or until it thickens slightly. Return the prawns to the wok for 1–2 minutes, or until heated and cooked through. Garnish with the finely chopped spring onion. Serve immediately with rice or thin egg noodles.

Serves 4

Notes: Chinese rice wine has a rich sweetish taste. Use dry sherry if unavailable.
Chinese black vinegar is made from rice and has a sweet, mild taste. It is available in Asian food stores.

Chicken with Thai basil, chilli and cashews

750 g chicken breast or thigh fillets, cut into strips
2 stems lemon grass, white part only, finely chopped
3 small fresh red chillies, seeded and finely chopped
4 cloves garlic, crushed
1 tablespoon finely chopped fresh ginger
2 fresh coriander roots, finely chopped
2 tablespoons oil
100 g cashews
1½ tablespoons lime juice
2 tablespoons fish sauce
1½ tablespoons shaved palm sugar or soft brown sugar
2 cups (60 g) lightly packed fresh Thai basil
2 teaspoons cornflour mixed with 1 tablespoon water

Place the chicken in a large bowl with the lemon grass, chilli, garlic, ginger and coriander root. Mix together well.

Heat a wok over medium heat, add 1 teaspoon of the oil and swirl to coat the surface of the wok. Add the cashews and cook for 1 minute, or until lightly golden. Remove and drain on paper towels.

Heat the remaining oil in the wok, add the chicken in batches and stir-fry over medium heat for 4–5 minutes, or until browned. Return the chicken to the wok.

Stir in the lime juice, fish sauce, palm sugar and basil, and cook for 30–60 seconds, or until the basil just begins to wilt. Add the cornflour mixture and stir until the mixture thickens slightly. Stir in the cashews and serve with steamed rice.

Serves 4

Phad Thai

250 g flat dried rice stick noodles
1 small fresh red chilli, chopped
2 cloves garlic, chopped
2 spring onions, sliced
1 tablespoon tamarind purée,
 combined with 1 tablespoon water
1½ tablespoons sugar
2 tablespoons fish sauce
2 tablespoons lime juice
2 tablespoons oil
2 eggs, beaten
150 g pork fillet, thinly sliced
8 raw large prawns, peeled, deveined
 and tails intact
100 g fried tofu, julienned
1 cup (90 g) bean sprouts
¼ cup (40 g) chopped roasted
 peanuts
3 tablespoons fresh coriander leaves
1 lime, cut into wedges

Soak the noodles in warm water
for 10 minutes. Drain.

Pound the chilli, garlic and spring
onion in a mortar and pestle.
Gradually blend in the tamarind
mixture, sugar, fish sauce and
lime juice.

Heat a wok until very hot, add
1 tablespoon of the oil and swirl
to coat. Add the egg, swirl to coat
and cook for 1–2 minutes, or until
set and cooked. Remove and shred.

Heat the remaining oil, stir in the chilli
mixture, and stir-fry for 30 seconds.
Add the pork fillet and stir-fry for
2 minutes, or until tender. Add the
prawns and stir-fry for 1 minute more.
Stir in the noodles, egg, tofu and half
the bean sprouts, and toss until
heated through.

Serve immediately topped with
the peanuts, coriander, lime and
remaining bean sprouts.

Serves 4–6

Japanese pork and noodle stir-fry

350 g pork fillet
1/3 cup (80 ml) soy sauce
1/4 cup (60 ml) mirin
2 teaspoons grated fresh ginger
2 cloves garlic, crushed
1 1/2 tablespoons soft brown sugar
500 g Hokkien noodles
2 tablespoons peanut oil
1 onion, cut into thin wedges
1 red capsicum, cut into thin strips
2 carrots, finely sliced on the diagonal
4 spring onions, finely sliced on the
   diagonal
200 g fresh shiitake mushrooms,
   sliced

Trim the pork of any excess fat or sinew and slice thinly. Combine the soy sauce, mirin, ginger, garlic and sugar in a large non-metallic bowl, add the pork and coat. Cover with plastic wrap and refrigerate for 10 minutes.

Meanwhile, place the noodles in a bowl of hot water for 5 minutes to separate and soften.

Heat a large wok over high heat, add 1 tablespoon oil and swirl to coat. Drain the pork, reserving the marinade, and stir-fry in batches for 3 minutes, or until browned. Remove and keep warm.

Reheat the wok over high heat, add the remaining oil and swirl to coat. Add the onion, capsicum and carrot, and stir-fry for 2–3 minutes, or until just tender, then add the spring onion and shiitake mushrooms. Cook for another 2 minutes, then return the pork to the wok. Drain the noodles and add to the wok with the reserved marinade. Toss to combine and cook for another 1 minute, or until heated through, then serve.

Serves 4

Family beef stir-fry

2 tablespoons peanut oil
350 g beef fillet, partially frozen and
  thinly sliced
1 large onion, cut into thin wedges
1 red capsicum, cut into thin strips
1 large carrot, thinly sliced on the
  diagonal
100 g snow peas, sliced in half
  diagonally
150 g baby corn, sliced in half
  diagonally
200 g straw mushrooms, drained
2 tablespoons oyster sauce
1 clove garlic, crushed
1 teaspoon grated fresh ginger
2 tablespoons light soy sauce
2 tablespoons medium sherry
1 tablespoon honey
1 teaspoon sesame oil
2 teaspoons cornflour

Heat a wok over high heat, add 1 tablespoon of the peanut oil and swirl around to coat the side of the wok. Add the meat in batches and cook for 2–3 minutes, or until nicely browned. Remove the meat from the wok and keep warm.

Heat the remaining peanut oil in the wok, add the onion, capsicum and carrot, and cook, stirring, for 2–3 minutes, or until the vegetables are just tender. Add the snow peas, corn and straw mushrooms, cook for a further minute, then return all the meat to the wok.

Combine the oyster sauce with the garlic, ginger, soy sauce, sherry, honey, sesame oil and 1 tablespoon water in a small bowl, then add the mixture to the wok. Mix the cornflour with 1 tablespoon of water, add to the wok and cook for 1 minute, or until the sauce thickens. Season to taste with salt and freshly ground black pepper. Serve immediately with rice or thin egg noodles.

Serves 4

Pork and brown bean noodles

3 tablespoons brown bean sauce
2 tablespoons hoisin sauce
3/4 cup (180 ml) chicken stock
1/2 teaspoon sugar
2 tablespoons peanut oil
3 cloves garlic, finely chopped
6 spring onions, sliced, white
  and green parts separated
650 g pork mince
500 g fresh Shanghai noodles
1 telegraph cucumber, halved
  lengthways, seeded and sliced
  on the diagonal
1 cup (30 g) fresh coriander leaves
1 cup (90 g) bean sprouts
1 tablespoon lime juice

Combine the brown bean and hoisin sauces, stock and sugar until smooth.

Heat the oil in a wok or large frying pan. Add the garlic and the white part of the spring onion, and cook for 10–20 seconds. Add the pork and cook over high heat for 2–3 minutes, or until it has changed colour. Add the bean mixture, reduce the heat and simmer for 7–8 minutes.

Cook the noodles in a large saucepan of boiling water for 4–5 minutes, or until tender. Drain and rinse, then divide among serving bowls. Toss together the cucumber, coriander, bean sprouts, lime juice and remaining spring onion. Spoon the sauce over the noodles and top with the cucumber mixture.

Serves 4–6

Stir-fried lamb with mint and chilli

1 tablespoon oil
750 g lamb fillet, thinly sliced
  (see Note)
4 cloves garlic, finely chopped
2 small fresh red chillies, thinly sliced
1/3 cup (80 ml) oyster sauce
2 1/2 tablespoons fish sauce
1 1/2 teaspoons sugar
1/2 cup (25 g) chopped fresh mint
1/4 cup (5 g) whole fresh mint leaves

Heat a wok over high heat, add the oil and swirl to coat. Add the lamb and garlic in batches and stir-fry for 1–2 minutes, or until the lamb is almost cooked. Return all the lamb to the wok. Stir in the chilli, oyster sauce, fish sauce, sugar and the chopped mint leaves, and cook for another 1–2 minutes.

Remove from the heat, fold in the whole mint leaves and serve immediately with rice.

Serves 4

Note: Make sure you slice the lamb across the grain—this will minimise the meat breaking up and shrinking when cooking.

Minced chicken salad

1 tablespoon jasmine rice
2 teaspoons oil
400 g chicken mince
2 tablespoons fish sauce
1 stem lemon grass, white part only,
  finely chopped
1/3 cup (80 ml) chicken stock
3 tablespoons lime juice
4 spring onions, finely sliced on
  the diagonal
4 red Asian shallots, sliced
1/2 cup (25 g) finely chopped fresh
  coriander leaves
1/2 cup (25 g) shredded fresh mint
200 g lettuce leaves, shredded
1/4 cup (40 g) chopped roasted
  unsalted peanuts
1 small fresh red chilli, sliced
lime wedges, to serve

Heat a frying pan. Add the rice and
dry-fry over low heat for 3 minutes,
or until lightly golden. Grind in a
mortar and pestle to a fine powder.

Heat a wok over medium heat.
Add the oil and mince and cook
for 4 minutes, or until it changes
colour, breaking up any lumps.
Add the fish sauce, lemon grass
and stock and cook for a further
10 minutes. Cool.

Add the lime juice, spring onion,
Asian shallots, coriander, mint
and ground rice. Mix well.

Arrange the lettuce on a serving
platter and top with the chicken
mixture. Sprinkle with the nuts and
chilli, and serve with lime wedges.

Serves 6

Braised water spinach with tofu

500 g firm tofu (see Note)
¼ cup (60 ml) oil
1 clove garlic, chopped
2 cm x 2 cm piece fresh ginger,
    chopped
750 g water spinach, cut into
    4 cm lengths
2 tablespoons kecap manis
2 tablespoons soy sauce
1 tablespoon toasted sesame seeds

Drain the tofu on paper towels and cut into 2 cm cubes. Heat a wok or large frying pan over high heat, add 2 tablespoons of the oil and swirl to coat the surface of the wok. Add the tofu and cook, turning occasionally, for 5 minutes, or until lightly browned. Drain on crumpled paper towels.

Heat the remaining oil in the wok, add the chopped garlic and ginger and stir-fry for 1 minute. Stir in the water spinach, kecap manis, soy sauce and 1 tablespoon water, toss well, then add the tofu and gently stir for 1 minute, or until the water spinach has wilted. Sprinkle with the sesame seeds and serve immediately with rice.

Serves 4

Note: To reduce cooking time you can use pre-fried tofu if available. Variation: Any leafy Asian green or English spinach can replace the water spinach.

Yakiudon

5 dried shiitake mushrooms
1 clove garlic, crushed
2 teaspoons grated fresh ginger
½ cup (125 ml) Japanese soy sauce
2 tablespoons rice wine vinegar
2 tablespoons sugar
1 tablespoon lemon juice
500 g fresh udon noodles
2 tablespoons oil
500 g chicken thigh fillets, thinly
  sliced
1 clove garlic, extra, finely chopped
1 small red capsicum, thinly sliced
2 cups (150 g) shredded cabbage
4 spring onions, thinly sliced
1 tablespoon sesame oil
white pepper, to taste
2 tablespoons drained shredded
  pickled ginger

Place the mushrooms in a heatproof bowl and soak in boiling water for 10 minutes, or until tender. Drain, reserving ¼ cup (60 ml) of the liquid. Discard the stems, squeeze the caps dry and thinly slice.

Combine the crushed garlic, ginger, soy sauce, vinegar, sugar, lemon juice and reserved soaking liquid.

Place the noodles in a heatproof bowl, cover with boiling water and leave for 2 minutes, or until soft and tender. Drain.

Heat a wok over high heat, add half the oil and swirl to coat. Add the chicken in batches and stir-fry for 5 minutes, or until browned. Remove from the wok.

Add the remaining oil and swirl to coat. Add the extra chopped garlic, mushrooms, capsicum and cabbage, and stir-fry for 2–3 minutes, or until softened. Add the noodles and stir-fry for another minute. Return the chicken to the wok and add the spring onion, sesame oil and soy sauce mixture, stirring until well combined and heated through. Season with white pepper and scatter with the pickled ginger.

Serves 4

Sweet pork

850 g pork spareribs
1/2 cup (125 g) grated palm sugar
  or soft brown sugar
4 red Asian shallots, sliced
1 tablespoon fish sauce
1 tablespoon kecap manis
1/2 teaspoon white pepper
1/3 cup (10 g) loosely packed fresh
  coriander leaves

Remove the bone and outer rind from the ribs. Cut into 1 cm slices.

Place the sugar in a wok with 2 tablespoons water and stir over low heat until the sugar dissolves. Increase to medium heat and boil, without stirring, for 5 minutes, or until the sugar turns an even, golden brown. Add the pork and shallots and stir to coat. Add the fish sauce, kecap manis, pepper and 1 cup (250 ml) warm water. Stir until any hard bits of sugar have melted.

Cover and cook for 10 minutes, stirring occasionally, then cook, uncovered and stirring often, for 20–30 minutes, or until the sauce is sticky and the meat is cooked. Garnish with coriander and serve with rice.

Serves 4–6

Stir-fried scallops with sugar snap peas

2 tablespoons oil
2 large cloves garlic, crushed
3 teaspoons finely chopped
   fresh ginger
300 g sugar snap peas
500 g scallops without roe,
   membrane removed
2 spring onions, cut into 2 cm
   lengths
2½ tablespoons oyster sauce
2 teaspoons soy sauce
½ teaspoon sesame oil
2 teaspoons sugar

Heat a wok over medium heat, add the oil and swirl to coat the surface of the wok. Add the garlic and ginger, and stir-fry for 30 seconds, or until fragrant.

Add the peas to the wok and cook for 1 minute, then add the scallops and spring onion and cook for 1 minute, or until the spring onion is wilted. Stir in the oyster and soy sauces, sesame oil and sugar and heat for 1 minute, or until warmed through. Serve with rice.

Serves 4

Chinese beef and broccoli stir-fry

¼ cup (60 ml) peanut oil
1 kg fresh rice noodle rolls, cut into
 2 cm strips, separated
500 g rump steak, trimmed and
 thinly sliced
1 onion, cut into wedges
4 cloves garlic, chopped
400 g Chinese broccoli, cut into
 3 cm lengths
1 tablespoon soy sauce
¼ cup (60 ml) kecap manis
1 small fresh red chilli, chopped
½ cup (125 ml) beef stock

Heat a wok over medium heat, add
2 tablespoons of the peanut oil and
swirl to coat the side of the wok.
Add the noodles and stir-fry gently
for 2 minutes. Remove from the wok.

Reheat the wok over high heat, add
the remaining oil and swirl to coat.
Add the beef in batches and cook
for 3 minutes, or until it is browned.
Remove from the wok. Add the onion
and stir-fry for 1–2 minutes, then add
the garlic and cook for a further
30 seconds.

Return all the beef to the wok and
add the Chinese broccoli, soy sauce,
kecap manis, chilli and beef stock,
and cook over medium heat for
2–3 minutes. Divide the rice noodles
among four large serving bowls
and top with the beef mixture.
Serve immediately.

Serves 4

Note: The noodles may break up
during cooking. This will not affect
the flavour of the dish.

Singapore noodles

375 g thin fresh egg noodles
10 g dried Chinese mushrooms
2½ teaspoons sugar
1½ tablespoons soy sauce
2 tablespoons Chinese rice wine
1½ tablespoons Indian madras
  curry powder
150 ml coconut milk
½ cup (125 ml) chicken stock
2 eggs
1 tablespoon sesame oil
3 tablespoons vegetable oil
2 cloves garlic, finely chopped
1 tablespoon finely chopped fresh
  ginger
2 small fresh red chillies, seeded
  and finely chopped
3 spring onions, sliced
300 g small raw prawns, peeled,
  deveined and halved
150 g Chinese roast pork, thinly
  sliced
120 g frozen peas
fresh coriander, to garnish

Cook the noodles in boiling salted water for 1 minute. Drain and rinse in cold water.

Soak the mushrooms in a bowl with ½ cup (125 ml) hot water for 10 minutes. Drain and reserve the liquid, then discard the hard stalks and finely slice the caps. Combine the reserved liquid with the sugar, soy sauce, rice wine, curry powder, coconut milk and stock. Lightly beat the eggs and sesame oil together.

Heat a wok and add 2 tablespoons of the oil. Cook the garlic, ginger, chilli and mushrooms for 30 seconds. Add the spring onion, prawns, roast pork, peas and noodles. Stir in the mushroom liquid mixture. Add the egg mixture in a thin stream and toss until warmed through. Serve in deep bowls, garnished with fresh coriander leaves.

Serves 4

Pork and mushroom with white pepper

15 g dried black fungus
1 tablespoon peanut oil
350 g pork fillet, thinly sliced
4 cloves garlic, thinly sliced
3 red Asian shallots, finely sliced
1 carrot, finely sliced on the diagonal
6 spring onions, cut into 2.5 cm
  lengths
2 tablespoons fish sauce
2 tablespoons oyster sauce
1 teaspoon ground white pepper

Soak the black fungus in a bowl of boiling water for 20 minutes. Rinse, then cut into slices.

Heat a wok over medium heat, add the oil and swirl to coat. Add the pork, garlic and shallots and stir-fry for 30 seconds. Add the carrot and spring onion and stir-fry for 2–3 minutes, or until the pork is no longer pink.

Add the black fungus, fish and oyster sauces and ground white pepper and stir-fry for another minute. Serve hot with rice.

Serves 4

Lamb with hokkien noodles and sour sauce

450 g hokkien noodles
2 tablespoons vegetable oil
375 g lamb backstrap, thinly sliced
   against the grain
75 g red Asian shallots, peeled and
   thinly sliced
3 cloves garlic, crushed
2 teaspoons finely chopped fresh
   ginger
1 small fresh red chilli, seeded and
   finely chopped
1½ tablespoons red curry paste
125 g snow peas, trimmed and
   cut in half on the diagonal
1 small carrot, julienned
½ cup (125 ml) chicken stock
15 g grated palm sugar or soft
   brown sugar
1 tablespoon lime juice
small whole basil leaves, to garnish

Cover the noodles with boiling water and soak for 1 minute. Drain and set aside.

Heat 1 tablespoon of the oil in a wok and swirl to coat. Stir-fry the lamb in batches over high heat for 2–3 minutes, or until it just changes colour. Remove to a side plate.

Add the remaining oil, then the shallots, garlic, ginger and chilli and stir-fry for 1–2 minutes. Stir in the curry paste and cook for 1 minute. Add the snow peas, carrot and the lamb and combine. Cook over high heat, tossing often, for 1–2 minutes.

Add the stock, palm sugar and lime juice, toss to combine and cook for 2–3 minutes. Add the noodles and cook for 1 minute, or until heated through. Divide among serving bowls and garnish with the basil.

Serves 4–6

Noodles with beef

500 g unsliced fresh rice noodles
2 tablespoons peanut oil
2 eggs, lightly beaten
500 g rump steak, thinly sliced
3 tablespoons kecap manis
1 1/2 tablespoons soy sauce
1 1/2 tablespoons fish sauce
300 g Chinese broccoli, cut into
  5 cm lengths
1/4 teaspoon white pepper
lemon wedges, to serve

Cut the noodles lengthways into 2 cm strips. Gently separate the strips — run under cold water if necessary.

Heat a wok over medium heat, add 1 tablespoon oil and swirl to coat. Add the egg, swirl to coat and cook for 1–2 minutes, or until set. Remove and slice.

Reheat the wok over high heat, add the remaining oil and swirl to coat. Cook the beef in batches for 3 minutes, or until brown. Remove.

Reduce the heat to medium, add the noodles and cook for 2 minutes. Combine the kecap manis, soy and fish sauces. Add to the wok with the broccoli and white pepper, then stir-fry for 2 minutes. Return the egg and beef to the wok and cook for 3 minutes, or until the broccoli has wilted and the noodles are soft but not breaking. Serve with the lemon.

Serves 4–6

Note: Rice noodles should not be refrigerated, as they are very difficult to separate when cold.

Spicy eggplant stir-fry

1 tablespoon chilli bean sauce
2 tablespoons soy sauce
1 tablespoon rice wine vinegar
½ teaspoon sugar
¼ cup (60 ml) oil
500 g eggplant, cubed
1 onion, cut into thin wedges
1 large fresh red chilli, seeded,
   sliced diagonally
2 cloves garlic, crushed
½ cup (15 g) fresh coriander leaves

Place the chilli bean sauce, soy sauce, rice wine vinegar and sugar in a small bowl, and whisk together well.

Heat a wok or frying pan over high heat, add 1 tablespoon of oil and swirl to coat. Add half the eggplant and cook, stirring, for 3–4 minutes, or until lightly browned all over. Drain on crumpled paper towels. Repeat with another tablespoon of oil and the remaining eggplant.

Reheat the wok over high heat, add the remaining oil and swirl to coat. Add the onion, chilli and garlic, and cook over medium heat for 2 minutes. Return the eggplant to the wok, add the sauce and cook, covered, for 5 minutes. Remove from the heat and stir in the coriander leaves. Serve with rice.

Serves 4

Note: Chilli bean sauce is used in many Sichuan-style dishes. If unavailable, replace it with garlic chilli bean paste or sambal oelek, available from some supermarkets or Asian food stores.

Fried noodles with chicken, pork and prawn

900 g fresh flat rice noodle sheets,
  cut into 2 cm thick slices
100 ml oil
2 cloves garlic, finely chopped
1 tablespoon grated fresh ginger
70 g garlic chives, cut into
  5 cm lengths
½ barbecue chicken, flesh cut into
  1 cm slices
300 g Chinese barbecue pork fillet,
  cut into 1 cm slices
1 small fresh red chilli, chopped
12 large cooked prawns, peeled
  and deveined
2 cups (180 g) bean sprouts
100 g English spinach
2 eggs, beaten
2 teaspoons caster sugar
½ cup (125 ml) light soy sauce
2 tablespoons dark soy sauce
2 tablespoons fish sauce

Rinse the rice noodles under warm running water and carefully separate. Drain.

Heat a wok over high heat, add ¼ cup (60 ml) of the oil and swirl to coat. Add the garlic and ginger, and cook, stirring, for 30 seconds. Be careful not to burn. Then add the chives and cook, stirring, for 10 seconds.

Add the barbecue chicken, barbecue pork, chilli and prawns, and cook, stirring, for 2 minutes, then add the bean sprouts and spinach, and cook, stirring, for 1 minute.

Make a well in the centre of the mixture, add the egg and scramble for 1 minute, or until firm but not hard. Stir in the remaining oil, then add the rice noodles. Stir to combine. Add the combined caster sugar, light and dark soy sauce, and fish sauce, and stir-fry for 2–3 minutes, or until heated through. Season with pepper.

Serves 4

Prawn and snow pea stir-fry

1 ½ tablespoons peanut oil
3 cloves garlic, thinly sliced
1 stem lemon grass (white part only),
  finely chopped
1 ½ tablespoons thinly sliced fresh
  ginger
1 kg raw medium prawns, peeled and
  deveined, with tails intact
200 g snow peas, trimmed and cut
  into 3–4 strips lengthways
6 spring onions, cut into thin slices
  on the diagonal
75 g snow pea sprouts
1 tablespoon Chinese rice wine or
  dry sherry
1 tablespoon oyster sauce
1 tablespoon soy sauce

Heat a wok to very hot, add the oil and swirl to coat the side. Add the garlic, lemon grass and ginger and stir-fry for 1–2 minutes, or until fragrant. Add the prawns and cook for 2–3 minutes, or until pink and cooked.

Add the snow peas, spring onion, sprouts, rice wine, oyster and soy sauces and toss until heated through and the vegetables start to wilt.

Serves 4–6

Mee Grob

4 Chinese dried mushrooms
oil, for deep-frying
100 g dried rice vermicelli
100 g fried tofu, cut into matchsticks
4 cloves garlic, crushed
1 onion, chopped
1 chicken breast fillet, thinly sliced
8 green beans, sliced on the diagonal
6 spring onions, thinly sliced on the
  diagonal
8 raw prawns, peeled and deveined,
  tails intact
30 g bean sprouts
fresh coriander leaves, to garnish

Sauce
1 tablespoon soy sauce
3 tablespoons white vinegar
5 tablespoons sugar
3 tablespoons fish sauce
1 tablespoon sweet chilli sauce

Soak the mushrooms in boiling water for 20 minutes. Drain the mushrooms, discard the stems and thinly slice.

Fill a wok one third full of oil and heat to 180°C (350°F), or until a cube of bread browns in 15 seconds. Cook the vermicelli in small batches for 5 seconds, or until puffed and crispy. Drain well.

Add the tofu to the wok in batches and deep-fry for 1 minute, or until crisp. Drain. Carefully remove all but 2 tablespoons of oil.

Reheat the wok until very hot. Add the garlic and onion, and stir-fry for 1 minute. Add the chicken, beans mushrooms, and half the spring onion. Stir-fry for 2 minutes, or until the chicken has almost cooked through. Add the prawns and stir-fry for a further 2 minutes, or until they just turn pink.

Combine all the sauce ingredients and add to the wok. Stir-fry for 2 minutes, or until the meat and prawns are tender and the sauce is syrupy. Remove from the heat, and stir in the vermicelli, tofu and sprouts. Garnish with the coriander and remaining sliced spring onion.

Serves 4–6

Pork, asparagus and baby corn stir-fry

1 clove garlic, chopped
1 teaspoon grated fresh ginger
2 tablespoons soy sauce
1/4 teaspoon ground white pepper
1 tablespoon Chinese rice wine
600 g pork fillet, thinly sliced
1 tablespoon peanut oil
1 teaspoon sesame oil
6 fresh shiitake mushrooms,
  thinly sliced
150 g baby corn
100 g asparagus, cut into 4 cm
  lengths on the diagonal
2 tablespoons oyster sauce

Place the garlic, ginger, soy sauce, pepper and wine in a bowl and mix together well. Add all the pork and stir until it is well coated in the marinade.

Heat a wok over high heat, add half the oils and swirl to coat the side of the wok. Add half the pork mixture and stir-fry for about 2 minutes, or until the pork changes colour. Remove the pork from the wok. Repeat with the remaining oils and pork mixture.

Add the mushrooms, corn and asparagus to the wok and stir-fry for 2 minutes. Return the pork and any juices to the wok and stir in the oyster sauce. Cook, stirring, for another 2 minutes, or until it is evenly heated through. Divide among four plates and serve with rice.

Serves 4

Chicken braised with ginger and star anise

1 teaspoon Sichuan peppercorns
2 tablespoons peanut oil
3 cm x 2 cm fresh ginger, julienned
2 cloves garlic, chopped
1 kg chicken thigh fillets, cut in half
1/3 cup (80 ml) Chinese rice wine
1 tablespoon honey
1/4 cup (60 ml) light soy sauce
1 star anise

Heat a wok over medium heat, add the peppercorns and cook, stirring to prevent burning, for 2–4 minutes, or until fragrant. Remove and lightly crush with the back of a knife.

Reheat the wok, add the oil and swirl to coat. Add the ginger and garlic, and cook over low heat for 1–2 minutes, or until slightly golden. Add the chicken, increase the heat to medium and cook for 3 minutes, or until browned all over.

Add the peppercorns, wine, honey, soy sauce and star anise to the wok, reduce the heat to low and simmer, covered, for 20 minutes, or until the chicken is tender. Divide among four plates and serve with steamed rice.

Serves 4

Pork with plum sauce and choy sum

600 g choy sum, cut into 6 cm
  lengths
½ cup (125 ml) peanut oil
1 large onion, sliced
3 cloves garlic, finely chopped
2 teaspoons finely chopped fresh
  ginger
500 g pork loin, thinly sliced
2 tablespoons cornflour, seasoned
  with salt and pepper
¼ cup (60 ml) plum sauce
1½ tablespoons soy sauce
1 teaspoon sesame oil
2 tablespoons dry sherry or Chinese
  rice wine

Bring a large saucepan of lightly salted water to the boil, add the choy sum and cook for 2–3 minutes, or until the stems are crisp but still tender. Plunge into iced water to chill completely, then drain.

Heat a wok over high heat, add 1 tablespoon oil and swirl to coat. Add the onion, garlic and ginger and cook over medium heat for 3 minutes, or until softened. Remove from the wok.

Toss the pork in the seasoned cornflour to coat, shaking off any excess. Reheat the wok over high heat, add the remaining oil and swirl to coat. Add the pork in batches and cook for 3 minutes, or until golden on both sides. Remove.

Drain the oil from the wok and return the meat and any juices. Combine the plum sauce, soy sauce, sesame oil and sherry, and add to the wok. Cook over high heat for 2–3 minutes, then add the choy sum and return the onion mixture. Cook, stirring, for a further 2 minutes. Serve immediately with rice.

Serves 4

Chiang mai noodles

250 g fresh thin egg noodles
2 tablespoons oil
6 red Asian shallots, finely chopped
3 cloves garlic, crushed
1–2 small fresh red chillies, seeded
  and finely chopped
2–3 tablespoons red curry paste
375 g chicken breast fillet, cut into
  thin strips
2 tablespoons fish sauce
1 tablespoon grated palm sugar
3 cups (750 ml) coconut milk
1 tablespoon lime juice
1 cup (250 ml) chicken stock
4 spring onions, sliced, to garnish
1/3 cup (10 g) fresh coriander leaves,
  to garnish
fried red Asian shallot flakes, to
  garnish
purchased fried noodles, to garnish
fresh red chilli, finely diced, to garnish

Cook the noodles in a saucepan of boiling water according to the packet instructions. Drain, cover and set aside.

Heat a large wok over high heat, add the oil and swirl to coat. Add the shallots, garlic and chilli, and stir-fry for 3 minutes. Stir in the curry paste and stir-fry for 2 minutes. Add the chicken and stir-fry for 3 minutes, or until it changes colour.

Stir in the fish sauce, palm sugar, coconut milk, lime juice and stock. Reduce the heat and simmer over low heat for 5 minutes—do not boil.

To serve, divide the noodles among four deep serving bowls and spoon in the chicken mixture. Garnish with the spring onion, coriander, shallot flakes, noodles and chilli.

Serves 4

Vegetable and tofu puff stir-fry with barbecue pork

2 tablespoons peanut oil
1 tablespoon finely chopped fresh
   ginger
2 cloves garlic, chopped
200 g snow peas, halved diagonally
   if large
1 carrot, sliced on the diagonal
1 small red capsicum, thinly sliced
300 g bok choy, chopped
160 g fried tofu puffs, halved
400 g barbecue pork, thinly sliced
   (see Note)
2 tablespoons soy sauce
1/4 cup (60 ml) Chinese rice wine
2 tablespoons oyster sauce
1 fresh red chilli, finely chopped
8 spring onions, sliced on the
   diagonal

Heat a large wok or frying pan over high heat, add the oil and swirl to coat. Add the ginger and garlic, and cook for 30 seconds, or until fragrant. Add the snow peas, carrot capsicum and bok choy, and stir-fry for 2–3 minutes, or until just tender but still crisp. Add the tofu puffs and pork, and toss to combine.

Add the soy sauce, rice wine, oyster sauce and chilli, and stir until heated through. Stir in the spring onion and serve with jasmine rice.

Serves 4

Note: You can buy barbecue pork at Asian food stores or Chinese barbecue restaurants. It is already cooked and is usually found in the takeaway food section.

Braised vegetables with cashews

1 tablespoon peanut oil
2 cloves garlic, crushed
2 teaspoons grated fresh ginger
300 g choy sum, cut into 10 cm
   lengths
150 g baby corn, sliced in half on
   the diagonal
3/4 cup (185 ml) chicken or vegetable
   stock
200 g canned, drained bamboo
   shoots
150 g oyster mushrooms, sliced
   in half
2 teaspoons cornflour
2 tablespoons oyster sauce
2 teaspoons sesame oil
1 cup (90 g) bean sprouts
75 g roasted unsalted cashews

Heat a wok over medium heat, add the oil and swirl to coat. Add the garlic and ginger and stir-fry for 1 minute. Increase the heat to high, add the choy sum and baby corn and stir-fry for another minute.

Add the chicken stock and cook for 3–4 minutes, or until the choy sum stems are just tender. Add the bamboo shoots and mushrooms, and cook for 1 minute.

Place the cornflour and 1 tablespoon water in a bowl and mix together well. Stir into the vegetables with the oyster sauce. Cook for 1–2 minutes, or until the sauce is slightly thickened. Stir in the sesame oil and sprouts, and serve immediately on a bed of steamed rice sprinkled with the roasted cashews.

Serves 4

Chilli beef

¼ cup (60 ml) kecap manis
2½ teaspoons sambal oelek
2 cloves garlic, crushed
½ teaspoon ground coriander
1 tablespoon grated palm sugar
   or soft brown sugar
1 teaspoon sesame oil
400 g beef fillet, partially frozen,
   thinly sliced
1 tablespoon peanut oil
2 tablespoons chopped roasted
   peanuts
3 tablespoons chopped fresh
   coriander leaves

Combine the kecap manis, sambal oelek, crushed garlic, ground coriander, palm sugar, sesame oil and 2 tablespoons water in a large bowl. Add the beef slices and coat well. Cover with plastic wrap and refrigerate for 20 minutes.

Heat a wok over high heat, add the peanut oil and swirl to coat. Add the meat in batches, cooking each batch for 2–3 minutes, or until browned.

Arrange the beef on a serving platter, sprinkle with the chopped peanuts and fresh coriander, and serve with steamed rice.

Serves 4

Curries

Musaman beef curry

1 tablespoon tamarind pulp
2 tablespoons oil
750 g lean stewing beef, cubed
2 cups (500 ml) coconut milk
4 cardamom pods, bruised
2 cups (500 ml) coconut cream
2–3 tablespoons prepared Musaman
  curry paste
2 tablespoons fish sauce
8 pickling onions, peeled
8 baby potatoes, peeled
2 tablespoons grated palm sugar
  or soft brown sugar
1/2 cup (80 g) unsalted peanuts,
  roasted and ground

Combine the tamarind pulp and
1/2 cup (125 ml) boiling water, and
set aside to cool. Mash the pulp
with your fingertips to dissolve,
then strain, reserving the liquid.

Heat the oil in a wok. Add the beef
in batches and cook over high heat
for 5 minutes per batch, or until
browned. Reduce the heat, add the
coconut milk and cardamom pods,
and simmer for 1 hour, or until the
beef is tender. Remove the beef, then
strain and reserve the cooking liquid.

Heat the coconut cream in the wok
and stir in 2–3 tablespoons of the
curry paste. Cook for 10 minutes,
or until it 'cracks', or the oil separates
from the cream. Add the fish sauce,
onions, potatoes, beef mixture, palm
sugar, peanuts, tamarind water and
the reserved liquid. Simmer for
25–30 minutes.

Serves 4

Rogan josh

1 kg boned leg of lamb
1 tablespoon ghee or oil
2 onions, chopped
$\frac{1}{2}$ cup (125 g) plain yoghurt
1 teaspoon chilli powder
1 tablespoon ground coriander
2 teaspoons ground cumin
1 teaspoon ground cardamom
$\frac{1}{2}$ teaspoon ground cloves
1 teaspoon ground turmeric
3 cloves garlic, crushed
1 tablespoon grated fresh ginger
400 g can chopped tomatoes
$\frac{1}{4}$ cup (30 g) slivered almonds
1 teaspoon garam masala
chopped fresh coriander leaves,
   to garnish

Trim the lamb of any excess fat and sinew, and cut it into 2.5 cm cubes.

Heat the ghee in a large saucepan, add the onion and cook, stirring, for 5 minutes, or until soft. Stir in the yoghurt, chilli powder, coriander, cumin, cardamom, cloves, turmeric, garlic and ginger. Add the tomato and 1 teaspoon salt, and simmer for 5 minutes.

Add the lamb and stir until coated. Cover and cook over low heat, stirring occasionally, for 1–1$\frac{1}{2}$ hours, or until the lamb is tender. Remove the lid and simmer until the liquid thickens.

Meanwhile, toast the almonds in a dry frying pan over medium heat for 3–4 minutes, shaking the pan gently, until the nuts are golden brown. Remove from the pan at once to prevent them burning.

Add the garam masala to the curry and mix through well. Sprinkle the slivered almonds and coriander leaves over the top and serve.

Serves 4–6

Butter chicken

2 tablespoons peanut oil
1 kg chicken thigh fillets, quartered
60 g butter or ghee
2 teaspoons garam masala
2 teaspoons sweet paprika
2 teaspoons ground coriander
1 tablespoon finely chopped fresh
  ginger
1/4 teaspoon chilli powder
1 cinnamon stick
6 cardamom pods, bruised
350 g puréed tomatoes
1 tablespoon sugar
1/4 cup (60 g) plain yoghurt
1/2 cup (125 ml) cream
1 tablespoon lemon juice

Heat a wok until very hot, add 1 tablespoon oil and swirl to coat. Add half the chicken thigh fillets and stir-fry for 4 minutes, or until browned. Remove. Add extra oil, as needed, and cook the remaining chicken. Remove.

Reduce the heat, add the butter to the wok and melt. Add the garam masala, sweet paprika, coriander, ginger, chilli powder, cinnamon stick and cardamom pods, and stir-fry for 1 minute, or until fragrant. Return the chicken to the wok and mix to coat in the spices.

Add the tomato and sugar, and simmer, stirring, for 15 minutes, or until the chicken is tender and the sauce has thickened.

Add the yoghurt, cream and juice and simmer for 5 minutes, or until the sauce has thickened slightly. Serve with rice and pappadums.

Serves 4–6

Yellow curry with vegetables

Yellow curry paste
8 small dried red chillies
1 teaspoon black peppercorns
2 teaspoons coriander seeds
2 teaspoons cumin seeds
1 teaspoon ground turmeric
1 1/2 tablespoons chopped fresh
  galangal
5 cloves garlic, chopped
1 teaspoon grated fresh ginger
5 red Asian shallots, chopped
2 stems lemon grass, white part only,
  chopped
1 teaspoon shrimp paste
1 teaspoon finely chopped lime rind

2 tablespoons peanut oil
2 cups (500 ml) coconut cream
1/2 cup (125 ml) vegetable stock
150 g snake beans, cut into 3 cm
  lengths
150 g fresh baby corn
1 slender eggplant, cut into 1 cm
  slices
100 g cauliflower, cut into small
  florets
2 small zucchini, cut into 1 cm slices
1 small red capsicum, cut into 1 cm
  slices
1 1/2 tablespoons fish sauce
1 teaspoon grated palm sugar or soft
  brown sugar
1 small fresh red chilli, chopped,
  to garnish
fresh coriander leaves, to garnish

To make the curry paste, soak
the chillies in boiling water for
15 minutes. Drain and chop. Heat
a frying pan, add the peppercorns,
coriander seeds, cumin seeds and
turmeric, and dry-fry over medium
heat for 3 minutes. Transfer to a
mortar and pestle or food processor
and grind to a fine powder.

Place the ground spices, chilli,
galangal, garlic, ginger, shallots,
lemon grass and shrimp paste in
a mortar and pestle and pound
until smooth. Stir in the lime rind.

Heat a wok over medium heat,
add the oil and swirl to coat. Add
2 tablespoons of the curry paste
and cook for 1 minute. Add 1 cup
(250 ml) of coconut cream and cook
over medium heat for 10 minutes,
or until the mixture is thick and the
oil separates.

Add the stock, vegetables and
remaining coconut cream and cook
for 5 minutes, or until the vegetables
are tender, but still crisp. Stir in the
fish sauce and sugar and garnish
with the chilli and coriander.

Serves 4

Madras beef curry

1 tablespoon oil or ghee
1 onion, chopped
3–4 tablespoons Madras curry paste
1 kg skirt or chuck steak, trimmed
   and cut into 2.5 cm cubes
1/4 cup (60 g) tomato paste
1 cup (250 ml) beef stock

Heat the oil in a large frying pan, add the onion and cook over medium heat for 10 minutes, or until browned. Add the curry paste and stir for 1 minute, or until fragrant.

Add the meat and cook, stirring, until coated with the curry paste. Stir in the tomato paste and beef stock. Reduce the heat and simmer, covered, for 1 hour 15 minutes, and then uncovered for 15 minutes, or until the meat is tender.

Serves 4

Thai jungle curry prawns

Curry paste
10–12 dried red chillies
4 red Asian shallots, chopped
4 cloves garlic, sliced
1 stem lemon grass, white part only,
   sliced
1 tablespoon finely chopped fresh
   galangal
2 small coriander roots, chopped
1 tablespoon finely chopped fresh
   ginger
1 tablespoon shrimp paste,
   dry-roasted
¼ cup (60 ml) oil

1 tablespoon oil
1 clove garlic, crushed
¼ cup (40 g) ground candlenuts
1 tablespoon fish sauce
300 ml fish stock
1 tablespoon whisky
600 g raw prawns, peeled, deveined,
   tails intact
1 small carrot, slivered
200 g snake beans, cut into
   2 cm lengths
50 g bamboo shoots
3 kaffir lime leaves, crushed
fresh Thai basil leaves, to garnish

To make the curry paste, soak
the chillies in 1 cup (250 ml) boiling
water for 10 minutes, then drain and
place in a food processor with the
remaining curry paste ingredients.
Season with salt and white pepper,
and process to a smooth paste.

Heat a wok over medium heat,
add the oil and stir to coat the
side. Add 3 tablespoons of the
curry paste and the garlic and cook,
stirring constantly, for 5 minutes, or
until fragrant. Stir in the candlenuts,
fish sauce, stock, whisky, prawns,
vegetables and lime leaves, and
bring to the boil. Reduce the heat
and simmer for 5 minutes, or until
the prawns and vegetables are
cooked through. Garnish with the
Thai basil leaves and black pepper.

Serves 6

Goan pork curry

2 teaspoons cumin seeds
2 teaspoons black mustard seeds
1 teaspoon cardamom seeds
1 teaspoon ground turmeric
1 teaspoon ground cinnamon
½ teaspoon black peppercorns
6 whole cloves
5 small dried red chillies
⅓ cup (80 ml) white vinegar
1 tablespoon soft brown sugar
⅓ cup (80 ml) oil
1 large onion, chopped
6–8 cloves garlic, crushed
1 tablespoon finely grated fresh
  ginger
1.5 kg pork leg, cut into 3 cm cubes

Dry-fry the spices and chillies in a large frying pan for 2 minutes, or until fragrant. Place in a spice grinder or food processor and grind until finely ground. Transfer to a bowl and stir in the vinegar, sugar and 1 teaspoon salt to form a paste.

Heat half the oil in a large saucepan. Add the chopped onion and cook for 5 minutes, or until lightly golden. Place the onion in a food processor with 2 tablespoons cold water and process until smooth. Stir into the spice paste.

Place the garlic and ginger in a small bowl, mix together well and stir in 2 tablespoons water.

Heat the remaining oil in the pan over high heat. Add the cubed pork and cook in 3–4 batches for 8 minutes, or until well browned. Return all the meat to the pan and stir in the garlic and ginger mixture. Add the onion mixture and 1 cup (250 ml) hot water. Simmer, covered, for 1 hour, or until the pork is tender. Uncover, bring to the boil and cook, stirring frequently, for 10 minutes, or until the sauce reduces and thickens slightly. Serve with rice and pappadums.

Serves 6

Quick duck curry

1 kg Peking duck (see Note)
1 tablespoon oil
1 red onion, finely chopped
2 cloves garlic, crushed
1 fresh red chilli, seeded, chopped
1 tablespoon red curry paste
1 tablespoon smooth peanut butter
400 ml coconut milk
1¼ cups (315 ml) chicken stock
1 tablespoon lime juice
1 tablespoon fish sauce
2 tablespoons chopped fresh
   coriander leaves

Remove the skin and bones from the Peking duck and cut the meat into bite-size pieces.

Heat the oil in a saucepan over medium heat, add the onion and cook for 5 minutes. Add the garlic and chilli, and cook for 2 minutes. Stir in the curry paste and cook for 1–2 minutes, or until fragrant, then stir in the peanut butter.

Gradually whisk in the coconut milk and cook for 2 minutes, or until well combined. Add the stock, bring to the boil, then reduce the heat and simmer for 10 minutes. Add the duck and simmer for 10 minutes. Stir in the lime juice and fish sauce. Scatter the coriander over the top and serve with rice or noodles.

Serves 4

Note: Peking duck is available from Chinese barbecue and roast meat outlets. Leave the skin on the duck if preferred.

Panang beef

Paste

8–10 large dried red chillies
6 red Asian shallots, chopped
6 cloves garlic, chopped
1 teaspoon ground coriander
1 tablespoon ground cumin
1 teaspoon white pepper
2 stems lemon grass, white part only,
    bruised and sliced
1 tablespoon chopped fresh galangal
6 fresh coriander roots
2 teaspoons shrimp paste
2 tablespoons roasted peanuts

1 tablespoon peanut oil
400 ml coconut cream
1 kg round or blade steak, cut into
    1 cm slices
400 ml coconut milk
1/3 cup (90 g) crunchy peanut butter
4 fresh kaffir lime leaves
3 tablespoons lime juice
2 1/2 tablespoons fish sauce
3–4 tablespoons grated palm sugar
    or soft brown sugar
1 tablespoon chopped roasted
    peanuts, extra, to garnish
fresh Thai basil, to garnish

To make the paste, soak the chillies in a large bowl of boiling water for 15 minutes, or until soft. Remove the seeds and chop. Place in a food processor with the shallots, garlic, ground coriander, ground cumin, white pepper, lemon grass, galangal, coriander roots, shrimp paste and peanuts and process until smooth— add a little water if the paste is too thick.

Place the peanut oil and the thick coconut cream from the top of the can (reserve the rest) in a saucepan and cook over medium heat for 10 minutes, or until the oil separates. Add 6–8 tablespoons of the paste and cook, stirring, for 5–8 minutes, or until fragrant.

Add the beef, coconut milk, peanut butter, lime leaves and the reserved coconut cream. Cook for 8 minutes, or until the beef just starts to change colour. Reduce the heat and simmer for 1 hour, or until the beef is tender. Stir in the lime juice, fish sauce and sugar. Serve garnished with the peanuts and Thai basil.

Serves 4–6

Malaysian Nonya chicken curry

Curry paste
2 red onions, chopped
4 small fresh red chillies, seeded
  and sliced
4 cloves garlic, sliced
2 stems lemon grass, white part
  only, sliced
3 cm x 2 cm piece galangal, sliced
8 kaffir lime leaves, roughly chopped
1 teaspoon ground turmeric
½ teaspoon shrimp paste,
  dry-roasted

2 tablespoons oil
750 g chicken thigh fillets, cut
  into bite-size pieces
400 ml coconut milk
3 tablespoons tamarind purée
1 tablespoon fish sauce
3 kaffir lime leaves, shredded

To make the curry paste, place all of the ingredients in a food processor or blender and process to a thick paste.

Heat a wok or large saucepan over high heat, add the oil and swirl to coat the side. Add the curry paste and cook, stirring occasionally, over low heat for 8–10 minutes, or until fragrant. Add the chicken and stir-fry with the paste for 2–3 minutes.

Add the coconut milk, tamarind purée and fish sauce to the wok, and simmer, stirring occasionally, for 15–20 minutes, or until the chicken is tender. Garnish with the lime leaves. Serve with rice and steamed bok choy.

Serves 4

Lamb kofta

1 kg lamb mince
1 onion, finely chopped
2 small fresh green chillies, finely
  chopped
3 teaspoons grated fresh ginger
3 cloves garlic, crushed
1/3 cup (25 g) fresh breadcrumbs
1 egg, lightly beaten
1 teaspoon ground cardamom
2 tablespoons ghee or oil

Sauce
1 tablespoon ghee or oil
1 onion, sliced
1 fresh green chilli, finely chopped
3 teaspoons grated fresh ginger
2 cloves garlic, crushed
1 teaspoon ground turmeric
3 teaspoons ground coriander
2 teaspoons ground cumin
1 teaspoon chilli powder
2 tablespoons white vinegar
3/4 cup (185 g) plain yoghurt
1 1/4 cups (315 ml) coconut milk

Line a baking tray with baking paper or plastic wrap. Place the mince in a large bowl with the onion, chilli, ginger, garlic, breadcrumbs, egg and cardamom. Season and mix together. Roll level tablespoons of the mixture into balls, and place on the tray.

Heat the ghee in a large frying pan, add the meatballs in batches and cook over medium heat for 10 minutes, or until browned all over.

To make the sauce, heat the ghee in the same pan, add the onion, chilli, ginger, garlic and turmeric, and cook, stirring, over low heat for 8 minutes, or until the onion is soft. Add the coriander, cumin, chilli powder, vinegar, meatballs and 1 1/3 cups (330 ml) water, and stir gently. Simmer, covered, for 30 minutes. Stir in the combined yoghurt and coconut milk, and simmer, partially covered, for another 10 minutes. Serve with rice.

Serves 4–6

Yellow fish curry

150 ml vegetable stock
1 tablespoon ready-made yellow
  curry paste (see Note)
1 tablespoon tamarind purée
1 tablespoon grated palm sugar
  or soft brown sugar
1 1/2 tablespoons fish sauce
150 g green beans, trimmed and cut
  into 4 cm lengths
1 cup (140 g) sliced, canned bamboo
  shoots, rinsed and drained
400 ml coconut cream
400 g perch fillet, cubed
1 tablespoon lime juice
lime wedges, to serve
fresh coriander leaves, to garnish

Place the vegetable stock in a large saucepan and bring to the boil. Add the curry paste and cook, stirring, for 3–4 minutes, or until fragrant. Stir in the combined tamarind purée, palm sugar and 1 tablespoon of the fish sauce. Add the beans and bamboo shoots, and cook over medium heat for 3–5 minutes, or until the beans are almost tender.

Add the coconut cream and bring to the boil, then reduce the heat, add the fish and simmer for 3–5 minutes, or until the fish is just cooked. Stir in the lime juice and remaining fish sauce. Garnish with the lime wedges and coriander leaves. Serve with rice.

Serves 4

Note: Yellow curry paste can be bought at supermarkets and Asian food stores.

Chickpea curry

1 cup (220 g) dried chickpeas
2 tablespoons oil
2 onions, finely chopped
2 large ripe tomatoes, chopped
1/2 teaspoon ground coriander
1 teaspoon ground cumin
1 teaspoon chilli powder
1/4 teaspoon ground turmeric
1 tablespoon channa (chole) masala
  (see Note)
20 g ghee or butter
1 small onion, sliced
fresh mint and coriander leaves,
  to garnish

Place the chickpeas in a bowl, cover with water and leave to soak overnight. Drain, rinse and place in a large saucepan. Cover with plenty of water and bring to the boil, then reduce the heat and simmer for 40 minutes, or until soft. Drain.

Heat the oil in a large saucepan, add the onion and cook over medium heat for 15 minutes, or until golden brown. Add the tomato, ground coriander and cumin, chilli powder, turmeric and channa (chole) masala, and 2 cups (500 ml) water, and cook for 10 minutes, or until the tomato is soft. Add the chickpeas, season well with salt and cook for 7–10 minutes, or until the sauce thickens. Transfer to a serving dish. Place the ghee or butter on top and allow to melt before serving. Garnish with the sliced onion, and the mint and coriander leaves.

Serves 6

Note: Channa (chole) masala is a spice blend specifically used in this dish. It is available at Indian grocery stores. Garam masala can be used as a substitute if it is unavailable, but this will alter the final flavour.

Green chicken curry

Curry paste
$1/2$ teaspoon cumin seeds, toasted
1 teaspoon coriander seeds, toasted
$1/4$ teaspoon white peppercorns
5 fresh coriander roots
3 tablespoons chopped fresh
  galangal
10 fresh long green chillies, chopped
1 stem lemon grass, chopped
6 red Asian shallots
3 cloves garlic, peeled
1 tablespoon shrimp paste
1 teaspoon grated kaffir lime or
  lime rind
2 tablespoons peanut oil

1 cup (250 ml) thick coconut cream
500 g chicken thigh fillets, thinly
  sliced
2 cups (500 ml) coconut milk
125 g snake beans, cut into 3 cm
  lengths
150 g broccoli, cut into small florets
1 tablespoon shaved palm sugar
  or soft brown sugar
2–3 tablespoons fish sauce
5 tablespoons fresh coriander leaves

To make the curry paste, place
the cumin seeds, coriander seeds
and peppercorns in a spice grinder
or mortar and pestle and grind into
a fine powder. Place the powder in a
food processor with $1/4$ teaspoon salt
and the remaining paste ingredients
and process until smooth.

Place the coconut cream in a wok,
bring to the boil over high heat and
cook for 10 minutes, or until the oil
separates, giving a thicker curry.

Reduce the heat to medium. Stir
in half the curry paste and cook
for 2–3 minutes, or until fragrant.
Add the chicken pieces and cook
for 3–4 minutes, or until almost
cooked. Stir in the coconut milk,
beans and broccoli. Bring to the
boil, then reduce the heat and
simmer for 4–5 minutes, or until
the chicken and vegetables are
cooked. Stir in the palm sugar,
fish sauce and coriander. Serve
with steamed rice and garnish with
extra coriander leaves, if desired.

Serves 4

Note: Store any leftover paste in
an airtight container in the freezer
for up to 3 months.

Fish ball curry

1 large onion, chopped
1 teaspoon sambal oelek
1 tablespoon finely chopped fresh
  ginger
1 stem lemon grass, white part only,
  finely chopped
3 tablespoons fresh chopped
  coriander roots
½ teaspoon ground cardamom
1 tablespoon tomato paste
1 tablespoon oil
1 tablespoon fish sauce
2 cups (500 ml) coconut milk
750 g fish balls (if frozen, thawed)
3 tablespoons chopped fresh
  coriander
fresh coriander, extra, to garnish

Place the onion, sambal oelek, ginger, lemon grass, coriander, cardamom and tomato paste in a food processor, and process to a smooth paste.

Heat the oil in a large saucepan. Add the spice paste and cook, stirring, over medium heat for 4 minutes, or until fragrant.

Stir in the fish sauce, coconut milk and 2 cups (500 ml) water. Bring to the boil, then reduce the heat and simmer for 15 minutes, or until the sauce has reduced and thickened slightly.

Add the fish balls and cook for 2 minutes. Do not overcook or the fish balls will be tough and rubbery. Stir in the coriander and garnish with extra coriander. Serve with rice.

Serves 6

Indian-style butter prawns

1 kg large raw prawns
100 g butter
2 large cloves garlic, crushed
1 teaspoon ground cumin
1 teaspoon paprika
1½ teaspoons garam masala
2 tablespoons good-quality
  ready-made tandoori paste
2 tablespoons tomato paste
300 ml thick cream
1 teaspoon sugar
⅓ cup (90 g) plain yoghurt
2 tablespoons chopped fresh
  coriander leaves
1 tablespoon flaked almonds,
  toasted
lemon wedges, to serve

Peel and devein the prawns, leaving the tails intact. Melt the butter in a large saucepan over medium heat, then add the garlic, cumin, paprika and 1 teaspoon of the garam masala and cook for 1 minute, or until fragrant. Add the tandoori paste and tomato paste, and cook for a further 2 minutes. Stir in the cream and sugar, then reduce the heat and simmer for 10 minutes, or until the sauce thickens slightly.

Add the prawns to the pan and cook for 8–10 minutes, or until they are pink and cooked through. Remove the pan from the heat and stir in the yoghurt, the remaining garam masala and half the coriander. Season.

Garnish with the flaked almonds and remaining coriander and serve with steamed rice and lemon wedges.

Serves 4

Note: This dish is very rich so we recommend that you serve it with steamed vegetables or a fresh salad.

Thai beef and pumpkin curry

2 tablespoons oil
750 g blade steak, thinly sliced
  (see Note)
4 tablespoons Musaman curry paste
2 cloves garlic, finely chopped
1 onion, sliced lengthways
6 curry leaves, torn
3 cups (750 ml) coconut milk
3 cups (450 g) butternut pumpkin,
  roughly diced
2 tablespoons chopped unsalted
  peanuts
1 tablespoon palm sugar
2 tablespoons tamarind purée
2 tablespoons fish sauce
curry leaves, to garnish

Heat a wok or frying pan over high heat. Add the oil and swirl to coat the side. Add the meat in batches and cook for 5 minutes, or until browned. Remove the meat from the wok.

Add the curry paste, garlic, onion and curry leaves to the wok, and stir to coat. Return the meat to the wok and cook, stirring, over medium heat for 2 minutes.

Add the coconut milk to the wok, then reduce the heat and simmer for 45 minutes. Add the diced pumpkin and simmer for 25–30 minutes, or until the meat and the vegetables are tender and the sauce has thickened.

Stir in the peanuts, palm sugar, tamarind purée and fish sauce, and simmer for 1 minute. Garnish with curry leaves. Serve with pickled vegetables and rice.

Serves 6

Note: Cut the meat into 5 x 5 x 2 cm pieces, then cut across the grain at a 45° angle into 5 mm thick slices.

Lamb korma

2 tablespoons blanched almonds
2 teaspoons grated fresh ginger
4 cloves garlic, crushed
1/2 teaspoon ground cinnamon
1/2 teaspoon ground cardamom
1/4 teaspoon ground cloves
1/2 teaspoon chilli powder
1/2 teaspoon ground mace
1 1/2 teaspoons paprika
1 teaspoon ground coriander
1/3 cup (80 g) ghee
2 onions, thinly sliced
1 kg boned leg of lamb, cubed
1/4 teaspoon saffron threads, soaked
   in 1 tablespoon warm water
1 cup (250 g) plain yoghurt
1/2 cup (125 g) sour cream
fresh coriander sprigs, to garnish

Place the almonds, ginger and garlic in a blender with 1/4 cup (60 ml) water. Blend until smooth. Add the ground spices, and blend for 10 seconds, or until combined.

Heat the ghee in a casserole dish, add the onion and cook over medium heat for 10–15 minutes, or until caramelised. Add the spice paste and cook, stirring to prevent sticking, for 5 minutes, or until fragrant.

Add the meat and toss to coat in the spices. Cook, stirring, for 5 minutes, or until browned.

Add the saffron and soaking liquid, half the yoghurt and half the sour cream. Season with salt and bring to the boil, then reduce the heat and simmer, covered, for 2 hours, or until the meat is tender. Stir frequently to prevent sticking, as the curry is quite dry when cooked. Skim any fat from the surface. Stir in the remaining yoghurt and sour cream, and garnish with the coriander. Serve with rice.

Serves 4–6

Chicken curry with apricots

18 dried apricots
1 tablespoon ghee
2 x 1.5 kg chickens, jointed
3 onions, finely sliced
1 teaspoon grated fresh ginger
3 cloves garlic, crushed
3 large fresh green chillies, seeded
  and finely chopped
1 teaspoon cumin seeds
1 teaspoon chilli powder
½ teaspoon ground turmeric
4 cardamom pods, bruised
4 large tomatoes, peeled and cut
  into eighths

Soak the dried apricots in 1 cup
(250 ml) hot water for 1 hour.

Melt the ghee in a large saucepan,
add the chicken in batches and
cook over high heat for 5–6 minutes,
or until browned. Remove from the
pan. Add the onion and cook, stirring
often, for 10 minutes, or until the
onion has softened and turned
golden brown.

Add the ginger, garlic and chopped
green chilli, and cook, stirring, for
2 minutes. Stir in the cumin seeds,
chilli powder and ground turmeric,
and cook for a further 1 minute.

Return the chicken to the pan,
add the cardamom, tomato and
apricots, with any remaining liquid,
and mix well. Simmer, covered, for
35 minutes, or until the chicken
is tender.

Remove the chicken, cover and keep
warm. Bring the liquid to the boil and
boil rapidly, uncovered, for 5 minutes,
or until it has thickened slightly.
Spoon the liquid over the chicken
and serve with steamed rice mixed
with raisins, grated carrot and
toasted flaked almonds.

Serves 6–8

Light red seafood curry

Chu chee paste
10 large dried red chillies
1 tablespoon shrimp paste
1 tablespoon white peppercorns
1 teaspoon coriander seeds
2 teaspoons finely grated kaffir lime
  rind
10 fresh kaffir lime leaves, finely
  shredded
1 tablespoon chopped fresh
  coriander stem
1 stem lemon grass, white part only,
  finely chopped
3 tablespoons chopped fresh galangal
6 cloves garlic, chopped
10 red Asian shallots, chopped

2 x 270 ml cans coconut cream
500 g raw medium king prawns,
  peeled, deveined and tails intact
500 g scallops, without roe
2–3 tablespoons fish sauce
2–3 tablespoons grated palm sugar
  or soft brown sugar
8 fresh kaffir lime leaves, finely
  shredded
2 small fresh red chillies, thinly sliced,
  optional
1 cup (30 g) fresh Thai basil

Soak the chillies in hot water
for 15 minutes. Drain, remove the
seeds and chop. Preheat the oven
to moderate 180°C (350°F/Gas 4).
Put the shrimp paste, peppercorns
and coriander seeds on a foil-lined
baking tray and bake for 5 minutes.

Blend the baked spices in a food
processor with the remaining paste
ingredients until smooth.

Remove 1 cup (250 ml) thick coconut
cream from the top of the cans
(reserve the rest) and place in a
wok. Heat until just boiling, then
stir in 3 tablespoons of the curry
paste. Reduce the heat. Simmer
for 10 minutes, or until fragrant
and the oil begins to separate.

Stir in the seafood and remaining
coconut cream and cook for
5 minutes. Add the fish sauce,
sugar, lime leaves and chilli and
cook for 1 minute. Stir in half the
basil and use the rest to garnish.

Serves 4

Paneer and pea curry

Paneer
2 litres full-cream milk
⅓ cup (80 ml) lemon juice
oil, for deep-frying

Curry paste
2 large onions
3 cloves garlic
1 teaspoon grated fresh ginger
1 teaspoon cumin seeds
3 dried red chillies
1 teaspoon cardamom seeds
4 cloves
1 teaspoon fennel seeds
2 pieces cassia bark

500 g frozen peas
2 tablespoons oil
400 g puréed tomatoes
1 tablespoon garam masala
1 teaspoon ground coriander
¼ teaspoon ground turmeric
1 tablespoon cream
fresh coriander leaves, to garnish

Bring the milk to the boil in a large saucepan, stir in the lemon juice and turn off the heat. Stir the mixture for 1–2 seconds as it curdles. Place in a colander and leave for 30 minutes for the whey to drain off. Place the paneer curds on a clean, flat surface, cover with a plate, weigh down and leave for at least 4 hours.

To make the curry paste, place all the ingredients in a spice grinder and grind to a smooth paste.

Cut the solid paneer into 2 cm cubes. Fill a deep, heavy-based saucepan one-third full of oil and heat to 180°C (350°F), or until a cube of bread browns in 15 seconds. Cook the paneer in batches for 2 minutes per batch, or until golden. Drain on paper towels. Bring a saucepan of water to the boil, add the peas and cook for 3 minutes, or until tender. Drain.

Heat the oil in a large saucepan, add the curry paste and cook over medium heat for 4 minutes, or until fragrant. Add the puréed tomato, spices, cream and ½ cup (125 ml) water. Season with salt and simmer for 5 minutes. Add the paneer and peas and cook for 3 minutes. Garnish with coriander leaves and serve hot.

Serves 6

Beef rendang

1 kg topside beef, cut into 1 cm
   thick strips
2 onions, chopped
1 tablespoon chopped fresh ginger
3 cloves garlic, finely chopped
1 teaspoon ground turmeric
2 teaspoons ground coriander
2½ tablespoons sambal oelek
100 ml oil
400 ml coconut cream
6 fresh curry leaves
1 stem lemon grass, bruised
100 ml tamarind purée
4 kaffir lime leaves
1 teaspoon soft brown sugar
1 kaffir lime leaf, extra, shredded,
   to garnish

Season the beef with salt and
white pepper. Place the onion,
ginger, garlic, turmeric, coriander
and sambal oelek in a blender, and
blend until smooth. Add a little water
if necesary.

Heat the oil in a large saucepan,
add the spice paste and cook over
medium heat for 5 minutes, or until
fragrant. Add the beef, stir to coat in
the spices and cook for 1–2 minutes.
Add the coconut cream, curry leaves,
lemon grass, tamarind purée, lime
leaves and 2 cups (500 ml) water.
Reduce the heat and simmer over
low heat for 2 hours 30 minutes,
or until the meat is tender and the
sauce has thickened. Add a little
water, if necessary, to prevent the
sauce sticking. Stir in the sugar.
Garnish with the shredded kaffir
lime leaf and serve with rice.

Serves 4

Malaysian hot and sour pineapple curry

1 half-ripe pineapple, cored,
 cut into chunks
1/2 teaspoon ground turmeric
1 star anise
7 cloves
1 cinnamon stick, broken into
 small pieces
7 cardamom pods, bruised
1 tablespoon oil
1 onion, finely chopped
1 teaspoon grated fresh ginger
1 clove garlic
5 fresh red chillies, chopped
1 tablespoon sugar
1/4 cup (60 ml) coconut cream

Place the pineapple in a saucepan, cover with water and add the ground turmeric. Wrap the star anise, cloves, cinnamon and cardamom pods in a square of muslin, and tie securely with string. Add to the pan and cook over medium heat for 10 minutes. Squeeze the bag to extract any flavour, then discard.

Heat the oil in a frying pan, add the onion, ginger, garlic and chilli, and cook, stirring, for 1–2 minutes, or until fragrant. Add the pineapple, and the cooking liquid, sugar and salt to taste. Cook for 2 minutes, then stir in the coconut cream. Cook, stirring, over low heat for 3–5 minutes, or until the sauce thickens. Serve hot or cold.

Serves 6

Note: This dish is very popular with children due to its colour and sweetness, but you might want to cut back on the chilli! If your pineapple is too ripe, this dish will turn to mush, so it is important to make sure you use a half-ripe pineapple that will keep its shape during cooking.

Sri Lankan chicken curry with cashews

Curry powder
3 tablespoons coriander seeds
1 1/2 tablespoons cumin seeds
1 teaspoon fennel seeds
1/4 teaspoon fenugreek seeds
2 cm cinnamon stick
6 cloves
1/4 teaspoon cardamom seeds
2 teaspoons dried curry leaves
2 small dried red chillies

2 tablespoons oil
1 kg chicken thigh fillets, trimmed, cut in half
1 onion, chopped
2 cloves garlic, crushed
2 teaspoons finely grated fresh ginger
1 teaspoon ground turmeric
2 x 415 g cans whole peeled tomatoes
165 ml coconut milk
1/2 cup (80 g) roasted cashew nuts

Dry-fry the coriander, cumin, fennel and fenugreek seeds separately over low heat until fragrant. Make sure the spices are well browned, not burnt. Place the browned seeds in a food processor, blender or mortar and pestle, add the remaining ingredients and process or grind to a powder.

Heat the oil in a large frying pan. Cook the chicken in batches for 10 minutes, or until browned all over. Remove and drain on paper towels.

Drain all but 1 tablespoon of oil from the pan. Add the onion, garlic, ginger and turmeric, and cook for 10 minutes, or until the onion is soft. Add 2 tablespoons of the curry powder and cook, stirring, for 3 minutes, or until fragrant.

Add the tomato and 1/2 teaspoon salt, bring to the boil, then reduce heat and simmer. Return the chicken to the pan and stir until coated with the sauce. Simmer, covered, for 15 minutes, then uncovered for 15 minutes, or until the chicken is tender and the sauce has thickened. Stir in the coconut milk and simmer for 3 minutes. Garnish with the cashews and serve with rice.

Serves 6

Red curry of roast pumpkin, beans and basil

600 g peeled and seeded pumpkin, cut into 3 cm cubes
2 tablespoons oil
1 tablespoon ready-made red curry paste
400 ml coconut cream (see Note)
200 g green beans, cut into 3 cm lengths
2 kaffir lime leaves, crushed
1 tablespoon grated light palm sugar or soft brown sugar
1 tablespoon fish sauce
1 cup (30 g) fresh Thai basil leaves, plus extra to garnish
1 tablespoon lime juice

Preheat the oven to moderately hot 200°C (400°F/Gas 6). Place the pumpkin in a baking dish with 1 tablespoon oil and toss to coat. Bake for 20 minutes, or until tender.

Heat the remaining oil in a saucepan, add the curry paste and cook, stirring constantly, breaking up with a fork, over medium heat for 1–2 minutes. Add the coconut cream ½ cup (125 ml) at a time, stirring with a wooden spoon between each addition for a creamy consistency. Then add the pumpkin and any roasting juices, the beans and kaffir lime leaves. Reduce the heat to low and cook for 5 minutes.

Stir in the palm sugar, fish sauce, basil and lime juice. Garnish with extra basil leaves. Serve with rice.

Serves 4

Note: If you want to make this a less fattening meal, use lite coconut cream instead of the full-fat version; the texture will be slightly different but the flavour of the curry will still be good.

One pots

Moroccan vegetable stew with minty couscous

2 tablespoons olive oil
1 onion, finely chopped
3 cloves garlic, finely chopped
1 teaspoon ground ginger
1 teaspoon ground turmeric
2 teaspoons ground cumin
2 teaspoons ground cinnamon
1/2 teaspoon dried chilli flakes
400 g can diced tomatoes
400 g can chickpeas, rinsed and drained
1/2 cup (80 g) sultanas
400 g butternut pumpkin, peeled and cut into 3 cm cubes
2 large zucchini (250 g), cut into 2 cm pieces
2 carrots, cut into 2 cm pieces
1 cup (185 g) instant couscous
25 g butter
4 tablespoons chopped fresh mint

Heat the olive oil in a large saucepan over medium heat. Add the onion and cook for 3–5 minutes, or until translucent but not brown. Add the garlic, ginger, turmeric, cumin, cinnamon and chilli flakes, and cook for 1 minute. Add the tomato, chickpeas, sultanas and 1 cup (250 ml) water. Bring to the boil, then reduce the heat and simmer, covered, for 20 minutes. Add the pumpkin, zucchini and carrot, and cook for a further 20 minutes, or until the vegetables are tender. Season with salt and black pepper.

Place the couscous in a large, heatproof bowl. Cover with 1 cup (250 ml) boiling water and leave to stand for 5 minutes, or until all the water is absorbed. Fluff with a fork and stir in the butter and mint. Season with salt and ground black pepper, and serve with the stew.

Serves 4

Lamb tagine

1 tablespoon ground cumin
1 teaspoon ground ginger
$\frac{1}{2}$ teaspoon ground turmeric
1 teaspoon paprika
$\frac{1}{3}$ teaspoon ground cinnamon
2 cloves garlic, crushed
$\frac{1}{3}$ cup (80 ml) olive oil
1.5 kg diced lamb shoulder
2 onions, sliced
2 cups (500 ml) beef stock
2 tomatoes, peeled and chopped
$\frac{1}{2}$ teaspoon saffron threads
1 carrot, cut into matchsticks
$\frac{1}{2}$ cup (15 g) chopped fresh coriander
  leaves
1 cup (155 g) pitted Kalamata olives
1 teaspoon finely chopped rinsed
  preserved lemon rind (see Note)
2 cups (370 g) instant couscous
60 g butter
1$\frac{1}{2}$ tablespoons honey

Place the cumin, ginger, turmeric, paprika, cinnamon, crushed garlic, 2 tablespoons oil and 1 teaspoon salt in a large bowl. Mix together, add the lamb and toss to coat. Refrigerate for 2 hours.

Heat the remaining oil in a large casserole dish over medium heat, add the lamb in batches and cook for 5–6 minutes, or until browned. Return the meat to the dish, add the onion and cook for 1–2 minutes. Add the stock, tomato, saffron, carrot and coriander. Bring to the boil, then reduce the heat to low and cook, covered, for 1 hour. Add the olives and preserved lemon and cook, uncovered, for 30 minutes.

Place the couscous in a large heatproof bowl. Add 1$\frac{1}{2}$ cups (375 ml) boiling water and leave to stand for 3–5 minutes. Stir in the butter and fluff up with a fork. Season. Spoon into deep bowls, top with the tagine and drizzle with the honey.

Serves 4

Note: Only use the rinsed rind of preserved lemons. Discard the bitter pith and flesh.

Italian beef casserole with polenta dumplings

2 tablespoons olive oil
1 onion, sliced
2 cloves garlic, crushed
1 tablespoon plain flour
1 kg blade or chuck steak, cut into
  3 cm cubes
1½ cups (375 ml) beef stock
1 tablespoon chopped fresh oregano
2 x 425 g cans tomatoes
2 red capsicums, roasted, peeled
  and cut into strips
²/₃ cup (100 g) instant polenta
⅓ cup (90 g) ready-made pesto

Preheat the oven to slow 150°C (300°F/Gas 2). Heat the oil in a 4 litre flameproof casserole dish, add the onion and garlic, and cook over medium heat for 8 minutes, or until soft but not brown. Sprinkle the flour over the top and stir well. Add the beef, stock, oregano, tomato and capsicum, season and simmer for 15 minutes, then bake, covered, for 1 hour 30 minutes.

Place 300 ml water in a saucepan, bring to the boil, then reduce the heat and simmer. Pour in the polenta in a thin stream, season and cook, stirring, for 2 minutes, or until it thickens and comes away from the side of the pan. Remove and cool.

Shape the cooled polenta into 12 round dumplings, place on top of the casserole and bake, covered for 1 hour, and then uncovered for 20–30 minutes. Garnish with the pesto and serve.

Serves 4–6

Catalan fish stew

300 g red mullet fillets
400 g firm white fish fillets
300 g cleaned calamari
1.5 litres fish stock
⅓ cup (80 ml) olive oil
1 onion, chopped
6 cloves garlic, chopped
1 small fresh red chilli, chopped
1 teaspoon paprika
pinch saffron threads
150 ml white wine
425 g can crushed tomatoes
16 raw medium prawns, peeled,
  deveined, tails intact
2 tablespoons brandy
24 black mussels, cleaned
1 tablespoon chopped fresh parsley

Picada
2 tablespoons olive oil
2 slices day-old bread, cubed
2 cloves garlic
5 blanched almonds, toasted
2 tablespoons fresh flat-leaf parsley

Cut the fish and calamari into 4 cm pieces. Place the stock in a large saucepan and bring to the boil for 15 minutes, or until reduced by half.

To make the picada, heat the oil in a frying pan and cook the bread, stirring, for 2 minutes, or until golden, adding the garlic for the last minute. Place all of the ingredients in a food processor and process, adding stock to make a smooth paste.

Heat 2 tablespoons of the oil in a saucepan, add the onion, garlic, chilli and paprika, and cook, stirring, for 1 minute. Add the saffron, wine, tomatoes and stock. Bring to the boil, then reduce the heat and simmer. Heat the remaining oil in a frying pan and fry the fish and calamari for 3–5 minutes. Remove from the pan. Add the prawns, cook for 1 minute, then pour in the brandy. Carefully ignite the brandy and let the flames burn down. Remove from the pan.

Add the mussels to the pan and simmer, covered, for 2–3 minutes, or until opened. Discard any that do not open. Add all the seafood and the picada to the pan, stirring until the sauce has thickened and the seafood is cooked. Season, sprinkle with the parsley and serve.

Serves 6–8

Mediterranean chicken stew

1 teaspoon ground cumin
1 teaspoon ground coriander
1 teaspoon paprika
¼ teaspoon ground ginger
1.5 kg chicken thigh fillets, quartered
2 tablespoons olive oil
1 large onion, sliced
3 cloves garlic, finely chopped
2 teaspoons fresh oregano, chopped
1 cup (250 ml) dry white wine
420 g can crushed tomatoes
300 ml chicken stock
2 fresh bay leaves, crushed
¼ teaspoon saffron threads, soaked
  in 2 tablespoons warm water
¼ cup (40 g) good-quality pitted
  green olives
¼ cup (40 g) good-quality pitted
  black olives
½ preserved lemon, flesh removed
  and rind cut into fine slivers
3 tablespoons finely chopped fresh
  flat-leaf parsley
fresh basil sprigs, to garnish

Combine the cumin, coriander, paprika and ginger, and rub over the chicken pieces.

Heat the oil in a large saucepan. Add the chicken in batches and cook over medium heat for 5 minutes, or until browned. Remove from the pan.

Reduce the heat, add the onion and cook, stirring constantly, for 5 minutes, or until golden. Add the garlic and oregano, and cook for 2 minutes, then add the wine and cook for 6 minutes, or until nearly evaporated. Add the tomato, stock, bay leaves and saffron and soaking liquid, and bring to the boil. Return the chicken to the pan and season well. Reduce the heat and simmer, covered, for 30 minutes, or until the chicken is cooked through.

Stir in the olives and preserved lemon, and cook, uncovered, for 10 minutes. Stir in the parsley, garnish with the sprigs of basil and serve.

Serves 4–6

Note: This stew is delicious served with mashed potato. For extra flavour, stir some shredded fresh basil through the potato before serving.

Osso buco with gremolata

850 g veal shanks (osso buco)
2 tablespoons olive oil
1 large carrot, finely chopped
1 large onion, finely chopped
3 cloves garlic, crushed
1 cup (250 ml) dry white wine
1 bay leaf, crumbled
800 g canned diced tomatoes
1½ cups (375 ml) chicken stock

Gremolata
1 clove garlic, finely chopped
2 tablespoons finely chopped fresh
  parsley
1 teaspoon finely grated lemon rind
1 anchovy fillet, rinsed and finely
  chopped

Preheat the oven to slow 150°C
(300°F/Gas 2). Season the shanks.
Heat the oil over medium heat in
a flameproof casserole dish, add
the shanks and brown on all sides.
Remove. Add the carrot, onion and
garlic, and cook for 3–5 minutes,
or until softened. Stir in the wine
and bay leaf, and cook for 5 minutes,
or until reduced by half. Return the
shanks, and add the tomato and
stock. Bring to the boil. Cover,
place in the oven and cook, turning
the meat occasionally, for 1 hour
45 minutes–2 hours, or until the
meat is tender.

Remove the shanks and cool slightly.
Remove the meat from the bones
and chop coarsely. Push the marrow
out of the bones and discard the
bones. Return the meat and marrow
to the tomato sauce and cook on
the stovetop for 20 minutes, or until
reduced slightly. Season.

Combine the gremolata ingredients.

Serve the osso buco with gremolata,
and fettucine, if desired.

Serves 4

Chicken casserole with mustard and tarragon sauce

¼ cup (60 ml) olive oil
1 kg chicken thigh fillets, halved,
  then quartered
1 onion, finely chopped
1 leek, sliced
1 clove garlic, finely chopped
350 g button mushrooms, sliced
½ teaspoon dried tarragon
1½ cups (375 ml) chicken stock
¾ cup (185 ml) cream
2 teaspoons lemon juice
2 teaspoons Dijon mustard

Preheat the oven to moderate 180°C (350°F/Gas 4). Heat 1 tablespoon oil in a flameproof casserole dish over medium heat, and cook the chicken in two batches for 6–7 minutes each, or until golden. Remove from the dish and set aside.

Add the remaining oil to the dish and cook the onion, leek and garlic over medium heat for 5 minutes, or until soft. Add the mushrooms and cook for 5–7 minutes, or until they are soft and browned, and most of the liquid has evaporated. Add the tarragon, chicken stock, cream, lemon juice and mustard, bring to the boil and cook for 2 minutes. Return the chicken pieces to the dish and season well. Cover.

Place the casserole in the oven and cook for 1 hour, or until the sauce has reduced and thickened. Season to taste, and serve with boiled chat potatoes and a green salad.

Serves 4

Tofu stroganoff

2 tablespoons plain flour
1 tablespoon paprika
500 g firm tofu, cut into 1.5 cm
 cubes
1 tablespoon soy bean oil
2 teaspoons tomato paste
¼ cup (60 ml) dry sherry
2 cups (500 ml) vegetable stock
12 pickling onions, halved
1 clove garlic, crushed
225 g field mushrooms, cut into
 1 cm slices
3 tablespoons sour cream
sour cream, extra, to garnish
2 tablespoons chopped fresh
 chives

Combine the flour and paprika in a plastic bag and season well. Add the tofu and shake to coat.

Heat the oil in a frying pan. Add the tofu and cook over medium heat for 4 minutes, or until golden. Add the tomato paste and cook for another minute. Add 2 tablespoons of the sherry, cook for 30 seconds then transfer the tofu to a bowl. Keep any remaining flour in the pan.

Pour 1 cup (250 ml) of the stock into the pan and bring to the boil. Add the onion, garlic and mushrooms, reduce the heat to medium and simmer, covered, for 10 minutes. Return the tofu to the pan with the remaining sherry and remaining stock. Season to taste. Return to the boil, reduce the heat and simmer for 5 minutes, or until heated through and the sauce has thickened.

Remove the pan from the heat and stir a little of the sauce into the sour cream until smooth and of pouring consistency, add to the pan. Garnish with a dollop of the extra sour cream and sprinkle with the chopped chives. Serve with noodles or steamed rice.

Serves 4

Chilli con carne

1 tablespoon olive oil
1 onion, chopped
3 cloves garlic, crushed
2 tablespoons ground cumin
1½ teaspoons chilli powder
600 g beef mince
400 g can crushed tomatoes
2 tablespoons tomato paste
2 teaspoons dried oregano
1 teaspoon dried thyme
2 cups (500 ml) beef stock
1 teaspoon sugar
300 g can red kidney beans,
   rinsed and drained
1 cup (125 g) grated Cheddar
½ cup (125 g) sour cream
2 tablespoons finely chopped
   fresh coriander leaves
corn chips, to serve

Heat the oil in a large saucepan over medium heat, add the onion and cook for 5 minutes, or until starting to brown. Add the garlic, cumin, chilli powder and mince, and cook, stirring, for 5 minutes, or until the mince has changed colour. Break up any lumps with the back of a wooden spoon. Add the tomato, tomato paste, herbs, beef stock and sugar, and stir to combine. Reduce the heat to low and cook, stirring occasionally, for 1 hour, or until the sauce is rich and thick. Stir in the beans and cook for 2 minutes to heat through.

Divide the chilli con carne among six serving bowls, sprinkle with the cheese and top with a tablespoon of sour cream. Garnish with the coriander. Serve with corn chips or rice.

Serves 6

Bean and capsicum stew

1 cup (200 g) dried haricot beans
(see Note)
2 tablespoons olive oil
2 large cloves garlic, crushed
1 red onion, halved and cut into thin
wedges
1 red capsicum, cut into 1.5 cm
cubes
1 green capsicum, cut into
1.5 cm cubes
2 x 400 g cans chopped tomatoes
2 tablespoons tomato paste
2 cups (500 ml) vegetable stock
2 tablespoons chopped fresh basil
$^2/_3$ cup (125 g) Kalamata olives, pitted
1–2 teaspoons soft brown sugar

Put the beans in a large bowl, cover
with cold water and soak overnight.
Rinse well, then transfer to a large
saucepan, cover with cold water
and cook for 45 minutes, or until
just tender. Drain.

Heat the oil in a large saucepan.
Cook the garlic and onion over
medium heat for 2–3 minutes,
or until the onion is soft. Add the
red and green capsicum and cook
for a further 5 minutes.

Stir in the tomato, tomato paste,
stock and beans. Simmer, covered,
for 40 minutes, or until the beans
are cooked through. Stir in the basil,
olives and sugar. Season with salt
and black pepper. Serve hot with
crusty bread.

Serves 4–6

Note: 1 cup of dried haricot beans
yields about 2½ cups cooked beans.
You can use 2½ cups tinned haricot
or borlotti beans instead if you prefer.

Spicy sausage stew

2 tablespoons olive oil
8 Italian sausages (700 g), cut
  into 4 cm lengths
1 leek, finely sliced
1 red capsicum, seeded and
  chopped
425 g can chopped tomatoes
1/2 cup (125 ml) chicken stock
300 g can butter beans, rinsed
  and drained
1 1/3 cups (250 g) instant couscous
25 g butter, melted
2 tablespoons fresh flat-leaf parsley

Heat half the oil in a saucepan over medium heat, add the sausage and cook for 6 minutes, or until browned. Remove. Cook the sliced leek in the remaining oil over low heat for 10–12 minutes, or until soft. Add the capsicum and cook for 1–2 minutes. Return the sausage to the pan and stir in the tomato and stock. Bring to the boil, then reduce the heat and simmer for 30 minutes. Add the beans, season and stir for 1–2 minutes to heat through.

Place the couscous in a heatproof bowl with 1 1/3 cups (330 ml) boiling water and a pinch of salt. Leave for 5 minutes, fluff up and stir in the butter. Divide among four bowls and spoon on the stew. Garnish with the parsley.

Serves 4

Greek octopus in red wine stew

1 kg baby octopus
2 tablespoons olive oil
1 large onion, chopped
3 cloves garlic, crushed
1 bay leaf
3 cups (750 ml) red wine
1/4 cup (60 ml) red wine vinegar
400 g can crushed tomatoes
1 tablespoon tomato paste
1 tablespoon chopped fresh oregano
1/4 teaspoon ground cinnamon
small pinch ground cloves
1 teaspoon sugar
2 tablespoons finely chopped fresh
   flat-leaf parsley

Cut between the head and tentacles of the octopus, just below the eyes. Grasp the body and push the beak out and up through the centre of the tentacles with your fingers. Cut the eyes from the head by slicing a small round off. Discard the eye section. Carefully slit through one side, avoiding the ink sac, and remove any gut from inside. Rinse the octopus well under running water.

Heat the oil in a large saucepan, add the onion and cook over medium heat for 5 minutes, or until starting to brown. Add the garlic and bay leaf, and cook for 1 minute further. Add the octopus and stir to coat in the onion mixture.

Stir in the wine, vinegar, tomato, tomato paste, oregano, cinnamon, cloves and sugar. Bring to the boil, then reduce the heat and simmer for 1 hour, or until the octopus is tender and the sauce has thickened slightly. Stir in the parsley and season to taste with salt and ground black pepper. Serve with a Greek salad and crusty bread to mop up the delicious juices.

Serves 4–6

Asian-flavoured beef stew

2 tablespoons olive oil
1 kg chuck steak, cut into 3 cm
  cubes
1 large red onion, thickly sliced
3 cloves garlic, crushed
3 tablespoons tomato paste
1 cup (250 ml) red wine
2 cups (500 ml) beef stock
2 bay leaves, crushed
3 x 1.5 cm strips orange zest
1 star anise
1 teaspoon Sichuan peppercorns
1 teaspoon chopped fresh thyme
1 tablespoon chopped fresh
  rosemary
3 tablespoons chopped fresh
  coriander leaves

Heat 1 tablespoon oil in a large
saucepan, add the beef and cook
in batches over medium heat for
2 minutes, or until browned. Remove.

Heat the remaining oil, add the onion
and garlic and cook for 5 minutes.
Add the tomato paste, cook for
3 minutes, then stir in the wine
and cook for 2 minutes.

Return the meat to the pan and add
the stock, bay leaves, orange zest,
star anise, Sichuan peppercorns,
thyme and rosemary. Reduce the
heat to low and simmer, covered,
for 1 hour 30 minutes–2 hours, or
until tender. Remove the bay leaves
and zest. Stir in 2½ tablespoons
coriander and garnish with the
remainder. Serve with rice.

Serves 4

Chinese beef in soy

700 g chuck steak, trimmed and
　cut into 2 cm cubes
1/3 cup (80 ml) dark soy sauce
2 tablespoons honey
1 tablespoon rice vinegar
3 tablespoons soy bean oil
4 cloves garlic, chopped
8 spring onions, finely sliced
1 tablespoon finely grated fresh
　ginger
2 star anise
1/2 teaspoon ground cloves
1 1/2 cups (375 ml) beef stock
1/2 cup (125 ml) red wine
spring onions, extra, sliced,
　to garnish

Place the meat in a non-metallic dish.
Combine the soy sauce, honey and
vinegar in a small bowl, then pour
over the meat. Cover with plastic
wrap and marinate for at least
2 hours, or preferably overnight.
Drain, reserving the marinade,
and pat the cubes dry.

Place 1 tablespoon of the oil in
a saucepan and brown the meat
in 3 batches, for 3–4 minutes per
batch—add another tablespoon
of oil, if necessary. Remove the
meat. Add the remaining oil and fry
the garlic, spring onion, ginger, star
anise and cloves for 1–2 minutes,
or until fragrant.

Return all the meat to the pan, add
the reserved marinade, stock and
wine. Bring the liquid to the boil
and simmer, covered, for 1 hour
15 minutes. Cook, uncovered,
for 15 minutes, or until the sauce
is syrupy and the meat is tender.

Garnish with the extra sliced spring
onions and serve immediately with
steamed rice.

Serves 4

Mushroom ragu with polenta

10 g dried porcini mushrooms
25 g butter
1 tablespoon olive oil
4 cloves garlic, finely chopped
400 g mixed mushrooms (cap, shiitake, Swiss brown), sliced if large
1 cup (250 ml) red wine
2 cups (500 ml) beef stock
3 tablespoons finely chopped fresh parsley
2 teaspoons chopped fresh thyme
100 g enoki mushrooms
1 cup (150 g) polenta
40 g butter
1/3 cup (35 g) grated Parmesan

Soak the porcini in 3/4 cup (185 ml) warm water for 15 minutes. Drain and chop, reserving the soaking liquid.

Heat the butter and oil in a saucepan, add the garlic and cook over medium heat for 3 minutes. Add the mixed mushrooms and cook for 3 minutes. Stir in the red wine and cook for 5 minutes. Add the porcini, soaking liquid, stock and parsley. Cook over medium heat for 25 minutes, or until the liquid has reduced by half. Stir in the thyme and enoki and keep warm.

Meanwhile, bring 1 litre lightly salted water to the boil in a large saucepan, then reduce the heat to medium. Stir with a wooden spoon to form a whirlpool and add the polenta in a very thin stream. Cook, stirring, for 20 minutes, or until the polenta comes away from the side of the pan. Stir in the butter and Parmesan, and serve immediately with the ragu over the top.

Serves 4

Boston baked soy beans

500 g dried soy beans
2 onions, chopped
1 tablespoon treacle
$\frac{1}{4}$ cup (55 g) demerara sugar
3 teaspoons dried mustard
2 smoked pork hocks (about 600 g each)
2 tablespoons tomato sauce

Soak the soy beans in a large bowl of cold water for at least 8 hours, or preferably overnight. Drain. Place in a large saucepan and cover with fresh water. Bring to the boil and simmer for 2 hours—top up with water, if necessary. Drain and reserve 2 cups (500 ml) of the cooking liquid.

Preheat the oven to warm 160°C (315°F/Gas 2–3). Place the reserved cooking liquid in a 3.5 litre heavy-based casserole dish. Add the onion, treacle, demerara sugar, mustard and $\frac{1}{2}$ teaspoon black pepper. Bring slowly to the boil. Reduce the heat and simmer for 2 minutes.

Add the beans and pork hocks. Bake, covered, for 3 hours, stirring once or twice during cooking—add a little water, if necessary, to keep the beans covered with liquid. Stir in the tomato sauce and bake, uncovered, for a further 30 minutes.

Remove the meat and skim any fat off the surface of the beans. Roughly shred the meat and return to the bean mixture. Serve hot.

Serves 4–6

Irish beef hotpot

1 kg chuck steak, cut into 3 cm
 cubes
seasoned flour, to coat
2 tablespoons olive oil
2 large onions, sliced
2 cloves garlic, crushed
2 bay leaves
2 teaspoons chopped fresh thyme
1 tablespoon chopped fresh parsley
1½ cups (375 ml) beef stock
4 potatoes, cut into 3 cm cubes
2 carrots, cut into 2 cm pieces

Preheat the oven to warm 170°C
(325°F/Gas 3). Toss the meat in the
seasoned flour to coat. Heat the oil
in a frying pan over medium heat,
add the beef in batches and cook
for 4–5 minutes, or until browned.
Drain and place in a 4 litre flameproof
casserole dish.

Add the onion and garlic to the frying
pan and cook for 5 minutes, or until
softened and lightly golden. Add the
bay leaves, thyme and half the
parsley, stirring, then pour in the
stock, stirring to remove any
sediment stuck to the base or side
of the pan. Transfer the stock mixture
to the casserole dish, cover and bake
for 1 hour 30 minutes.

Add the potato and carrot to the
casserole dish, and add a little water,
if necessary. Return to the oven and
cook for 1 hour, or until the meat and
vegetables are tender. Garnish with
the remaining parsley.

Serves 4

Note: This dish is delicious if made
a day ahead and gently reheated.

Spanish-style chicken casserole

2 tablespoons light olive oil
750 g chicken thighs
750 g chicken drumsticks
1 large onion, chopped
2 cloves garlic, crushed
2 teaspoons sweet paprika
1 large red capsicum, sliced
200 ml dry sherry
415 g can peeled tomatoes
2 tablespoons tomato paste
3/4 cup (165 g) green olives, pitted, halved
1 teaspoon sweet paprika, extra

Preheat the oven to moderate 180°C (350°F/Gas 4). Heat the oil in a large frying pan, add the chicken in batches and cook over medium heat for 3–4 minutes, or until browned. Transfer to a 4 litre flameproof casserole dish. Add the onion, garlic, paprika and capsicum to the frying pan, and cook for 5–8 minutes, or until softened. Add the sherry and cook for 2 minutes, or until slightly reduced. Add the tomatoes and tomato paste, stir well and cook for 2 minutes. Pour the tomato mixture over the chicken and add 1 cup (250 ml) water.

Bake, covered, for 1 hour 15 minutes, then uncovered for 15 minutes. Add the olives and leave for 10 minutes. Garnish with the extra paprika and serve with rice.

Serves 4

Spicy vegetable stew with dhal

Dhal
¾ cup (165 g) yellow split peas
5 cm piece fresh ginger, grated
2–3 cloves garlic, crushed
1 fresh red chilli, seeded and
  chopped

3 tomatoes
2 tablespoons oil
1 teaspoon yellow mustard seeds
1 teaspoon cumin seeds
1 teaspoon ground cumin
½ teaspoon garam masala
1 red onion, cut into thin wedges
3 slender eggplants, cut into 2 cm
  slices
2 carrots, cut into 2 cm slices
¼ cauliflower, cut into florets
1½ cups (375 ml) vegetable stock
2 small zucchini, cut into 3 cm slices
½ cup (80 g) frozen peas
½ cup (15 g) fresh coriander leaves

To make the dhal, place the split peas in a bowl, cover with water and soak for 2 hours. Drain. Place in a large saucepan with the ginger, garlic, chilli and 3 cups (750 ml) water. Bring to the boil, then reduce the heat and simmer for 45 minutes, or until soft. Allow to cool slightly, then place in the bowl of a food processor or blender and process to a purée.

Score a cross in the base of the tomatoes, soak in boiling water for 2 minutes, then plunge into cold water and peel the skin away from the cross. Remove the seeds and roughly chop.

Heat the oil in a large saucepan. Cook the spices over medium heat for 30 seconds, or until fragrant. Add the onion and cook for a further 2 minutes, or until the onion is soft. Stir in the tomato, eggplant, carrot and cauliflower.

Add the dhal purée and stock, mix together well and simmer, covered, for 45 minutes, or until the vegetables are tender. Stir occasionally. Add the zucchini and peas during the last 10 minutes of cooking. Stir in the coriander leaves and serve hot.

Serves 4–6

Beef bourguignon

1 kg chuck steak, cut into
  3 cm cubes
seasoned flour, to coat
2 tablespoons oil
200 g bacon, chopped
30 g butter
150 g pickling onions
3 cloves garlic, finely chopped
1 leek, sliced
250 g button mushrooms
2 carrots, diced
3 tablespoons tomato paste
2 cups (500 ml) red wine
2 cups (500 ml) beef stock
2 teaspoons chopped fresh thyme
2 bay leaves
4 tablespoons finely chopped fresh
  flat-leaf parsley

Toss the meat in the flour to coat. Shake off any excess. Heat the oil in a large saucepan, add the bacon and cook over medium heat for 3–4 minutes, or until lightly browned. Remove from the pan. Add the beef in small batches and cook for 3–4 minutes, or until starting to brown. Remove from the pan.

Melt the butter in the pan, add the onions, garlic and leek, and cook for 4–5 minutes, or until softened.

Return the beef and bacon to the pan, add the remaining ingredients, except the parsley, and stir well. Bring to the boil, then reduce the heat and simmer, covered, stirring occasionally, for 1 hour, then uncovered for 30 minutes, or until the meat is very tender and the sauce thickened. Remove the bay leaves and stir in the parsley. Serve with mashed potato.

Serves 6

Pork and white bean chilli

1.3 kg pork shoulder, boned,
  trimmed and cut into 2 cm
  cubes (700–800 g meat)
2–3 tablespoons oil
1 large onion, diced
3 cloves garlic, finely chopped
1 tablespoon sweet paprika
1/2 teaspoon chilli powder
2 canned chipotle peppers or
  jalapeño chillies, chopped
1 tablespoon ground cumin
415 g can diced tomatoes
2 x 400 g cans cannellini beans,
  rinsed and drained
1 cup (30 g) fresh coriander
  leaves, coarsely chopped
sour cream, to serve
lime wedges, to serve

Season the pork. Heat 2 tablespoons oil in a large casserole dish over high heat. Add half the pork and cook for 5 minutes, or until brown. Remove. Repeat with the remaining pork, using more oil if necessary.

Lower the heat to medium, add the onion and garlic and cook for 3–5 minutes, or until soft. Add the paprika, chilli powder, chipotle peppers and cumin, and cook for 1 minute.

Return the pork to the pan. Add the tomato and 3 cups (750 ml) water and simmer, partially covered, for 1–1 1/2 hours, or until the pork is very tender. Add the beans and heat through. Boil a little longer to reduce the liquid if necessary. Stir in the coriander and season. Serve with sour cream and lime wedges.

Serves 4

Tamarind beef

2 tablespoons oil
1 kg chuck steak, cut into
  4 cm cubes
2 red onions, sliced
3 cloves garlic, finely chopped
1 tablespoon julienned fresh ginger
2 teaspoons ground coriander
2 teaspoons ground cumin
$1/2$ teaspoon ground fenugreek
$1/2$ teaspoon chilli powder
$1/2$ teaspoon ground cloves
1 cinnamon stick
$1/2$ cup (125 g) tamarind purée
6 fresh curry leaves
1 cup (250 ml) coconut cream
100 g green beans, halved
fresh coriander sprigs, to garnish

Heat the oil in a large saucepan, add the beef in batches and cook over high heat for 2–3 minutes, or until browned. Remove.

Add the onion and cook over medium heat for 3 minutes, or until soft, then add the garlic and ginger, and cook for a further 2 minutes. Add the coriander, cumin, fenugreek, chilli powder, cloves and cinnamon stick, and cook for 2 minutes.

Return the meat to the pan and stir to coat with the spices. Add the tamarind purée, curry leaves and $1 1/2$ cups (375 ml) water. Bring to the boil, then reduce the heat and simmer, covered, for 1 hour 30 minutes, or until the beef is tender. Add the coconut cream and cook, uncovered, for a further 10 minutes, then add the beans and cook for 5 minutes, or until tender but still crisp. Garnish with the coriander sprigs and serve with rice.

Serves 4

Cypriot pork and coriander stew

1 ½ tablespoons coriander seeds
800 g pork fillet, cut into 2 cm dice
1 tablespoon plain flour
¼ cup (60 ml) olive oil
1 large onion, thinly sliced
1 ½ cups (375 ml) red wine
1 cup (250 ml) chicken stock
1 teaspoon sugar
fresh coriander sprigs, to garnish

Crush the coriander seeds in a mortar and pestle. Combine the pork, crushed seeds and ½ teaspoon cracked pepper in a bowl. Cover and marinate overnight in the fridge.

Combine the flour and pork and toss. Heat 2 tablespoons oil in a frying pan and cook the pork in batches over high heat for 1–2 minutes, or until brown. Remove.

Heat the remaining oil, add the onion and cook over medium heat for 2–3 minutes, or until just golden. Return the meat to the pan, add the wine, stock and sugar, and season. Bring to the boil, then reduce the heat and simmer, covered, for 1 hour.

Remove the meat. Return the pan to the heat and boil over high heat for 3–5 minutes, or until reduced and slightly thickened. Pour over the meat and top with the coriander.

Serves 4–6

Goulash

100 g bacon, julienned
1 onion, chopped
2 tomatoes, peeled and chopped
1 clove garlic, chopped
½ teaspoon caraway seeds, lightly
  crushed
1½ tablespoons sweet paprika
1 kg lamb fillet, trimmed and cut
  into 2 cm pieces
1 bay leaf
1 cup (250 ml) vegetable stock
450 g chat potatoes, cut into
  2 cm pieces
100 g fresh or frozen peas
3 tablespoons sour cream
sweet paprika, extra, to garnish

Place the bacon in a 4 litre casserole dish and cook over medium heat for 4–5 minutes. Add the onion and cook for 2 minutes, then add the tomato and cook for 1 minute.

Stir in the garlic, caraway seeds, paprika, lamb, bay leaf and stock. Bring to the boil, then reduce the heat to low, and simmer, covered, for 40 minutes.

Add the potato and cook, uncovered, for 15 minutes, or until tender, then add the peas and cook for 5 minutes, or until tender. Stir in the sour cream and gently heat, without boiling. Garnish with paprika and serve with rye bread.

Serves 6

Chicken fricassée

25 g butter
1 tablespoon olive oil
200 g button mushrooms, sliced
1.5 kg chicken pieces
1 onion, chopped
2 sticks celery, sliced
1 cup (250 ml) dry white wine
1 cup (250 ml) chicken stock
1 fresh bay leaf
1 cup (250 ml) cream
1 kg King Edward or russet potatoes,
  peeled and chopped
$^2/_3$ cup (170 ml) milk, heated
70 g butter, extra
2 tablespoons chopped fresh parsley

Heat half the butter and oil in a large saucepan. Add the mushrooms and cook over medium heat for 5 minutes, or until soft and golden. Remove from the pan with a slotted spoon. Heat the remaining oil and butter, add the chicken pieces in batches and cook for 4 minutes, or until browned. Remove from the pan.

Add the onion and celery to the pan, and cook for 8 minutes, or until soft. Pour in the white wine and stir well. Add the stock, chicken, mushrooms, bay leaf and cream. Bring to the boil, then reduce the heat and simmer, covered, for 30–45 minutes, or until the chicken is cooked through and tender.

Meanwhile, bring a large saucepan of water to the boil, add the potato and cook for 10 minutes, or until tender. Drain, add the milk and extra butter, and mash with a potato masher until smooth. Season with salt and freshly ground black pepper.

Add the chopped parsley to the chicken and season. Serve with mashed potato.

Serves 4

Index

Photographers: Cris Cordeiro, Craig Cranko, Joe Filshie, Roberto Jean François, Ian Hofstetter, Andre Martin, Rob Reichenfeld, Brett Stevens

Food Stylists: Marie-Hélène Clauzon, Jane Collins, Sarah de Nardi, Georgina Dolling, Cherise Koch, Michelle Noerianto

Food Preparation: Alison Adams, Justine Johnson, Valli Little, Ben Masters, Kate Murdoch, Kim Passenger, Justine Poole, Christine Sheppard, Angela Tregonning

Published by Murdoch Books Pty Limited

Designer: Michelle Cutler (internals); Marylouise Brammer (cover)
Photographers: Jared Fowler (chapter openers); Stuart Scott (cover)
Stylists: Cherise Koch; (chapter openers); Louise Bickle (cover)
Editor: Gordana Trifunovic Production: Elizabeth Malcolm

Chief Executive: Juliet Rogers
Publishing Director: Kay Scarlett
Commissioning Editor: Lynn Lewis
Senior Designer: Heather Menzies

National Library of Australia Cataloguing-in-Publication Data
Title: Bowl food/editor, Lynn Lewis. ISBN 9781741964141 (pbk.)
Series: New chunky. Includes index. Subjects: Cookery. 641.8

Printed by 1010 Printing International Limited.
PRINTED IN CHINA
First printed 2003. This edition printed in 2009. Reprinted 2009 (twice).

For fan-forced ovens, set the oven temperature to 20°C (35°F) lower than indicated in the recipe.
We have used 20 ml tablespoon measures. IMPORTANT: Those who might be at risk from the effects
of salmonella poisoning (the elderly, pregnant women, young children and those suffering from immune
deficiency diseases) should consult their GP with any concerns about eating raw eggs.

Cover credits: Bread board, Dandi. Butter knife, Ici et la. Butter dish and soup
bowl, Beclau. Print tea towel, Prints Charming. Spot and floral print fabrics, Spotlight.
Front flap: Print fabric, Spotlight.

A catalogue record for this book is available from the British Library.

Published by:	UK
AUSTRALIA	Murdoch Books UK Ltd
Murdoch Books Pty Ltd	Erico House, 6th Floor North,
Pier 8/9, 23 Hickson Road,	93-99 Upper Richmond Rd,
Millers Point NSW 2000	Putney, London SW15 2TG
Phone: + 61 (0) 2 8220 2000	Phone: + 44 (0) 20 8785 5995
Fax: + 61 (0) 2 8220 2558	Fax: + 44 (0) 20 8785 5985
www.murdochbooks.com.au	www.murdochbooks.co.uk